The Lost Garden

Almost everyone I knew—whether they were white, yellow, or black—came from a single background. They were cut from one pattern of cloth. However, I was a bunch of different pieces that had been dumped together in a box by sheer circumstance.

I was the Chinese American raised in a black neighborhood, a child who had been too American to fit into Chinatown and too Chinese to fit in elsewhere. I was the clumsy son of the athletic family, the grandson of a Chinese grandmother who spoke more of West Virginia than of China.

THE
LOST
GARDEN

LAURENCE YEP

THE LOST GARDEN

A Beech Tree Paperback Book
New York

This edition is reprinted by arrangement with Simon & Schuster Books for
Young Readers, Simon & Schuster Children's Publishing Division.

Simon & Schuster, 1230 Avenue of the Americas, New York, NY 10020.
Printed in the United States of America.

Library of Congress Cataloging in Publication Data
Yep, Laurence.
The lost garden / by Laurence Yep. — 1st Beech Tree ed.
p. cm.
Summary: The author describes how he grew up as a Chinese American in San Francisco and
how he came to use his writing to celebrate his family and his ethnic heritage.
1. Yep, Laurence—Juvenile literature. 2. Authors, American—20th century—Biography—
Juvenile literature. 3. Chinese Americans—California—San Francisco—Social life and
customs—Juvenile literature. 4. Chinese Americans—California—San Francisco—Biography—
Juvenile literature. 5. San Francisco (Calif.)—Social life and customs—Juvenile literature.
6. San Francisco (Calif.)—Biography—Juvenile literature. [1. Yep, Laurence. 2. Authors,
American. 3. Chinese Americans—Biography.] I. Title.
PS3575.E6Z47 1996 979.4'610045102—dc20 [B] 95-53801 CIP AC
ISBN 0-688-13701-6

Originally published in 1991 by Julian Messner, a division of Simon & Schuster
First Beech Tree Edition, 1996
10 9

CONTENTS

To the Reverend John Becker, S.J., who started it all.

THE LOST GARDEN

YOUR FIRST *home will always be the one that you remember best. I have been away from it for over twenty years; and yet I still go back in my dreams.*

When my father died, I returned that night and for many nights to our old apartment and our store. I asked my mother about her dreams; and she said that she had also gone back there in her sleep.

I go back when I am troubled. I go back when I am especially at peace. It draws me as if it is a special magnet attracting my soul.

I finally went back to look at it after my father's death. We lived in an apartment on the corner of Pierce and Eddy streets right over our store in a neighborhood of San Francisco that was very ordinary for the fifties and sixties.

The apartment house that had been my home was gone now, its three stories torn down a year after I left for college in Milwaukee. It's been replaced by a two-story parking garage for the medical college up the block.

There were trees growing where the store door had been. I had to look at the street signs on the corner to make sure I was in the right spot. Behind the trees was a door of solid metal painted a battleship gray. Stretching to either side were concrete walls with metal grates bolted over the openings in the sides. The upper story of the garage was open to the air but through the grates I could look into the lower level. The gray, oil-stained concrete spread onward endlessly, having replaced the red cement floor of our store. Lines marked parking places where my parents had laid wooden planks to ease the ache and chill on their feet. Where the old-fashioned glass store counter had been was a row of expensive German cars.

As I walked beside the thick, impenetrable walls, I thought that it was more like a fortress for cars rather than a garage. A metal gate now stood where marble steps had once led up to the front door of our apartment. The gate itself had been shut with a rusty chain as if the doctors now used another entrance.

I looked past the steel I-beams that formed the columns and ceiling of the garage, peering through the dimness in an attempt to locate where my father's garden had been; but there was only an endless stretch of cars within the painted stalls.

We called it the garden though that was stretching the definition of the word because it was only a small, narrow cement courtyard on the northside of our apartment house. Trapped between the buildings there was only a brief time during the day when the sun could reach the tiny courtyard; but fuchsia bushes, which loved the shade, grew as tall as trees from the dirt plot there. Next to it my father had fashioned shelves from old hundred-pound rice cans and planks; and on those make-shift shelves he had his miniature flower patches growing in old soda *pop crates from which he had removed the wooden dividers. He would go out periodically to a wholesale nursery by the beach and load the car with boxes full of little flowers and seedlings which he would lovingly transplant in his shadowy garden.*

If you compared our crude little garden to your own backyards, you would probably laugh; and yet the cats in the neighborhood loved my father's garden almost as much as he did—to his great dismay. As just about the only green growing things in the area, the cats loved to roll among the flowers, crushing them in their ecstasy. Other times, they ate them—perhaps as a source of greens. Whatever the case, my father could have done without their destructive displays of appreciation.

I don't know where my father came by his love of growing things. He had come to San Francisco as a boy and, except for a brief time spent picking fruit, had lived most of his life among cement, brick, and asphalt. I hadn't thought of my father's garden in years; and yet it was the surest symbol of my father—beyond even a basketball because he was gardening long after he had given up playing and coaching. Somehow, he could persuade flowers to grow within the old, yellow Coca-Cola crates though the sun seldom touched them; and he could coax green shoots out of what seemed like lifeless sticks. His was the gift of renewal.

However, though I stared and stared, I could not quite figure out where it had been. Everything looked the same; more concrete and more cars. Store, home, and garden had all been torn down and replaced by something as cold, massive, and impersonal as a prison. Even if I could have gone through the gate, there was nothing for me inside there. If I wanted to return to that lost garden, I would have to go back into my own memories.

THE
LOST
GARDEN

I

THE
PEARL
APARTMENTS

YEARS AGO I wrote a book called *Child of the Owl*. It was about a little girl, Casey Young, who had grown up outside of San Francisco. When something happened to her father, she had to move into Chinatown to live with her grandmother. For the first time in her life, she had to think of herself as Chinese.

The title was symbolic of her situation—and of mine and of most Chinese Americans. In Western folklore, owls are usually wise animals. In Chinese folklore, on the other hand, owls are nasty animals. They are disrespectful to their parents and will even kick them out of the nest.

For the same act—such as reading comic books—Casey can feel just as wise as a Western owl and just as disrespectful as a Chinese one. In the late sixties, when I wore my hair long like many other college students, I knew my own grandmother,

Marie Lee, would have liked me to cut it short. Again, like so many other students at the time, I wasn't about to give in to convention.

To do my grandmother credit, she did not scold me or throw a tantrum the way many other grandmothers might have. Her solution was unique like much of what she did. As I sat talking with her in her little studio apartment, she would reach over abruptly and unannounced to brush the hair out of my eyes as a hint that it was time to visit the barber. I would try my best to ignore the gesture and go on talking.

I knew that she accepted her strange, American-born grandson—far better than I accepted my China-born grandmother. In many ways, she came to embody what I came to consider my "Chineseness"—that foreign, unassimilable, independent core. Going into Chinatown once a week made me learn about a part of myself that I sometimes wanted to ignore. For a while, she even lived with us while she was recuperating from an operation on her eyes so that for a short time I had to think about my "Chineseness" each day.

Like Casey, I grew up outside of Chinatown. At the end of World War II, my father had bought a small corner grocery and moved into an apartment above the store.

It was an older building so that it even came with a name: the Pearl Apartments. Officially, the Pearl Apartments sat at 1205 Pierce Street. The neighborhood was mixed—not only in people but in architectural styles. The houses were all different—Victorians and stucco postwar houses squatting side by side. However, the Pearl Apartments had their own colorful history. Initially the building had consisted of the store and two sets of apartments. But a second building of three apartments had been jacked up from another location and slowly and painfully brought to the corner where it was joined to the first building by a set of stairs.*

*When it was finally torn down to make room for the garage, it took two wrecking balls because it had been so sturdily built.

It wasn't a Victorian; but it pretended to be. The bay windows had panes of glass that curved outward—which were always a nuisance for my father to replace when I broke one of them. There was ornate molding on the walls that was great for catching dust; and chandeliers—cheap ones—hung from the ceiling by long chains through which the electric cord wound, its old insulation looking as fuzzy as a stretched-out caterpillar. I always thought of chandeliers as the corpses of fat spiders, their legs kicking up from their round, upturned bodies. They were great earthquake indicators, swaying whenever a tremor hit. However, they were handiest at New Year's because you could throw serpentines, coiled ribbons of paper, over them until there seemed to be a small tree of softly colored ribbons winding upward from the center of the living room floor.

The apartments each had certain features that had been modern once but were now old-fashioned. In the hallway was a little shelf and niche for the old type of phone—the kind that stands up like a candlestick—and each living room had a Murphy bed.

A Murphy bed swung up inside a closet on powerful springs. When the bed was up, it looked like a closet door. In our own apartment, my father had removed the Murphy bed, building instead a homemade captain's bed with drawers that pulled out underneath. The sides curved and over the edge he had put a strip of metal; and it is to that bed I often return in my dreams though I am sleeping some place far different now.

After scrimping and saving, my parents bought the Pearl Apartments, and my father decided to make some small improvements in the other residences. When my father was taking out the Murphy bed from the upstairs unit, one of the springs uncoiled and the sharp tip pierced his cheek. My father combined a steelworker's toughness with the impishness of a small boy, so until the wound healed, he liked to shock people by drinking some water and letting it dribble through the hole in his cheek.

The one drawback to the Pearl Apartments was that there was

no heating of any kind. My parents heated one end of the apartment by leaving the door down on the gas stove. The living room fireplace had to warm the other half; and one of my chores as a child was chopping up the old wooden fruit crates to use as firewood.

Often, I would lie there in the bed my father had made, snuggled under the many quilts for warmth, watching the shadows of the chandelier dance back and forth over the high ceiling as I slowly fell asleep.

Three flights up from the street was a metal door with a metal latch like some castle gate. Sometimes it stuck; but if you put your shoulder to it and shoved, it would open onto our windy, sun-washed roof.

It was up there my father had also built a sandbox for me, bringing the sand one armload at a time up the three flights of stairs. There I could play under the clotheslines that crossed overhead, their shadows dividing the rooftop into long, even strips. (Sometimes there would be a long line of purple silk boxer shorts handmade by our tenant Mrs. Pauloff for her son. They would flap stiffly like flags.)

Playing in the sandbox was the closest thing to flying. Standing in the sand, I would be high above all the other buildings, as if I were on a sea filled with rafts floating upward into the sky. There was usually a breeze blowing over the rooftop so that I had the illusion I was moving; and if it was a particularly windy day, the clouds would race overhead like huge-hulled, tall-masted yachts, increasing the illusion. Sometimes when I was older, I would dare to go near the edge feeling the electric tingle spread from my toes up my legs as I looked down from the dizzying heights.

It was a wonder that we never flew kites from the rooftop because we flew kites at almost every other windy spot in San Francisco. The Marina Green on the northern edge of San Francisco next to the bay was a favorite place because there were no trees. My father was the master of the winds. As he was fond of saying, a good kite flier shouldn't have to run to get a kite up. With his feet planted firmly in the grass and with just a puff of a breeze, he could coax a kite up high into the sky. In his garden, opposite the fuchsia plants, my father kept the long bamboo poles from which he fashioned kites whenever he had spare time. Since he usually made kites in the shape of butterflies, they were like pets that he teased upward with twitches and tugs of the string. (I usually had to run; and sometimes even that didn't work.)

My father made his kites from scratch, beginning with a section of bamboo that he would cut in half lengthwise with a small hand ax. He would repeat this process until he had long, slender rods that would bend where the now invisible joints had been. From these rods, he would fashion the outline of a butterfly, complete with wings and body and antennae.

To hold the rods together, my father used his own paste, which he made from ground-up rice and water, and strips of special rice paper that he purchased in a Chinatown stationery store where it lay in a dusty drawer. With larger sheets, he would cover the butterfly itself and then paint it with brightly colored poster paints.

Though I only saw him make butterfly kites, he also created other kites. The sparrow kites interested me the most since they were used for duels. In those battles, the kite string was dipped first into a bowl of rice paste and then into ground glass. The idea was to cut the string of your opponent and send his kite (in my father's time, it would have been men handling the sparrow kites) soaring free up into the clouds. That seems like a kinder and more poetic end than most losers receive—in fact, it hardly seems like a defeat at all except that money might be changing hands if betting is involved.

My father, Yep Gim Lew, or Thomas, was born in China in 1914 in the district of Toisan in the province of Kwangtung.

Toisan is a small county to the southwest of the ports of Canton and Hong Kong. Though there are some two million people living in the Toisan district today, there are an estimated four million Toisanese or those of Toisanese ancestry living abroad.

Even though my father was born in China, he had papers that said he was an American citizen because he was the son of a citizen. Immigration laws made it almost impossible for a Chinese to obtain the citizenship that was available to other groups so I'm not sure how his father became a citizen. It is possible that his father was helped by his Irish business partner.

When my father was ten, his father brought him to America. His father's first business had been a restaurant in El Paso. Many Chinese came over in 1849 to work in the gold fields of California and in the 1860s they helped build a railroad across the steep, snowy Sierras, linking the West Coast with the East Coast for the first time by rail. After the transcontinental railroad was built, Chinese then worked on the trunk lines that led to Los Angeles and from there across the Southwest. Some of the men would later settle in those areas. Or, since it was so hard to enter directly into America, there were many Chinese who went to Mexico first and later slipped over the border into America. In any case, I suspect, though I cannot say for sure, that my grandfather had some relatives who lived there. Seeking an opportunity, my grandfather tried to settle in Texas; but it was too hot, according to my father, so he eventually wound up in San Francisco.

It was in San Francisco that he became partners with an Irishman, Herbert Dugan, in the Dugan's pharmacy—which is strange enough. In the nineteenth century, the Chinese and the Irish had often been at one another's throats, competing for the same jobs and opportunities. When Mark Twain, the author of *The Adventures of Huckleberry Finn* and *The Adventures of Tom Sawyer*, had been a reporter in San Francisco, he had written about a Chinese being mugged by an Irishman while a policeman, also Irish, had simply watched. Because the newspaper had refused to print the story, Mark Twain quit—however, I should also add that his editor had his own version of why Mark Twain was fired.

Stranger still, the two new partners became friends so that they both lived in the same house and were taken care of by Dugan's sister. Dugan seemed to have been a man with a healthy appetite for living. He liked to go riding—I still have the big, broad leather belt he used. Dugan also had a wide range of friends—Jack London's widow was among his acquaintances. (Jack London was the author of such books as *Call of the Wild*.)

Through Dugan's connections, when my father arrived in America, he was not kept for very long by the immigration authorities on Angel Island, where so many Chinese were held and interrogated for months.

I still have a photo of my father at the age of ten. He is in pants that reach to his knees, called knickers, which most boys wore then; and he stares at the camera with a serious, frightened look, his hair cut short under his flat cap. He spent most of his first few months in America being beaten up by the white boys on the block; or, when the white boys weren't around, by the one Chinese boy who wanted to beat up someone else for a change. However, my father had a certain athletic ability; and he soon learned American games and sports and used them to make his enemies into friends.

My mother's family came from Yanping, a district next to Toisan; but my mother, Franche, was born in Lima, Ohio, in 1915 and raised in Clarksburg, West Virginia, and later in Bridgeport in the same state. By that time, there were Chinatowns in most of the country's major urban areas, including Pittsburgh; and geographically there is a link between the two areas.

Her father, Sing Thin Lee, seeking better business opportunities, wound up running a laundry in Clarksburg. In Clarksburg, there had once been a private school run by an old family, called the Davissons, who had been among the first Americans to settle in the area. Isabella ("Belle") Davisson ran her own private school, the Clarksburg Select School, in a building next to her home. Her niece, Miss Alcinda Marie Davisson, also taught some of the classes and continued to give music lessons in their home even after the school was closed. After the school was shut, it was rented out to enterprising Chinese who had started a laundry.

It was this business that my grandfather bought, moving his growing family down to Clarksburg where they were befriended by Miss Alcinda. They became such good friends that my grandmother took her American name, Marie, from Miss Alcinda's middle name; and my uncle, her only boy, was named Davisson. Later, my Auntie Susie was named after one of Miss Alcinda's friends, a fellow teacher by the name of Susan Mathilda Walker.

One of Miss Davisson's ancestors had been among the first American settlers in that area of West Virginia, later serving as a lieutenant in the Revolutionary War; and so a member of one of Clarksburg's oldest families befriended one of its newest families.

My mother grew up in the rolling green hills of Harrison County. Whenever I need to picture what it means when a person's face shines, I have only to picture my mother or her sister talking about West Virginia. They went sledding in the wintertime, dodged bulls in a farmer's pasture, looked for Indian arrowheads in creeks, and generally did whatever the white children did—including getting dosed with spring tonics. Under Miss Davisson's tutoring, my mother became an excellent speller so that she has proofread all of my books, catching many mistakes the computer misses.**

**Until I bought my first computer, my mother, a former secretary, also typed all my manuscripts with four carbons and an original.

However, when my mother was about ten, the family relocated to California. In San Francisco, my mother's family had hard times; and they were once reduced to eating lettuce sandwiches. Across the street was a shop that sold fish and shrimp. To earn a little extra money, the girls helped peel shrimp by the bucketload until eventually they became sick of the smell. They were glad when the store across the street hung out a sign announcing that there was no shrimp that day.

Besides the shock of moving from green hills to concrete ones, my mother also became the target of other children. She spoke both English and Chinese with a West Virginia twang. She also saw nothing wrong with playing basketball against the boys—much to the disgust of the old-time Chinese.

My father and mother met at Galileo High School, a school that overlooks the bay and has a football field so short that they cannot use the regular goalposts for points after a touchdown but have to use another set on the side.

Since my mother was also an athlete in track and basketball, they moved in the same circles and it was natural for them to get to know one another. (Though my mother is five feet four inches, she was tall for a Chinese girl in those days and was actually the center on her basketball team.) Among other things, they would go to the Golden Gate theater where a singer by the name of Lena Horne was performing in between movies.

By then, the Great Depression had begun and everyone was beginning to feel the pinch. By the time my parents graduated from high school, my mother's family was in even worse circumstances and my father's family was suffering, too. My father was able to go for one year to junior college, picking fruit in the summertime to help pay some bills.

Though a teenager, my father was strong enough to be invited to play football alongside grown men. In those days, the various Chinatowns had their own social clubs which fielded different teams. In one of the games, he broke his nose—

though even that didn't stop him. (Since his nose was never properly fixed, he would invite acquaintances to feel the little dip where the bone had not been set right.)

In high school, my mother had earned money by doing some simple housework. Eventually, my father, too, wound up in the domestic service as a houseboy. Even so, they would try to meet one another and ride home on the Sacramento Street cable car—there were a good deal more cable car lines in San Francisco in those days. Cable cars are vehicles pulled up the steep San Francisco hills by moving cables underneath the street.

Eventually, my father became a playground director in Chinatown. One of his proudest moments came when he took a group of boys—boys whose parents were too busy working to spend time with them, boys who were always the last to be picked for other teams (one boy even had a permanent limp)—and turned those boys into a championship basketball team.

By then, he and my mother were married and had a son Thomas—though few people called him that. When my brother was born in 1939, his hair stuck up straight so that he was nicknamed Spike. Another nickname came from a friend of the family. Since my father was named Gim in Chinese, Spike was also sometimes referred to as Gimlet.

During the war, my father worked as a welder at the shipyards; and toward the end of the war, he scraped together all their savings, borrowed money from family and friends, and bought a small corner grocery store out in an area of San Francisco known as the Western Addition, about a mile and a half away from the house where he had grown up as a boy.

Originally it had been a *taqueria*—a place that sold Mexican food—with big bins for flour and other items. Subsequently it had been converted into a grocery store by an Hispanic who proudly named it, "*La Conquista*," or The Conquest—I suppose after the conquest of Mexico by Cortés. However, since he was also a cab driver, he opened the store at such irregular hours that the customers never knew when it would be open.

Because they had no money to spare for luxuries such as signs, my parents kept the name La Conquista. Years later, Coca-Cola provided us with a free sign with their logo. Unfortunately, when the company put it up, we found the signmaker had misspelled our store's name. It was La Conquesta instead of La Conquista. However, by that time, everyone in the neighborhood called the store, Tom's, after my father. My mother was Mrs. Tom. My brother was Little Tom; and I was Baby Tom. Later, when my brother got married and moved away, I was sometimes called Little Tom.

When we bought the store, it was in a mixed neighborhood—white, Hispanic, black, and Asian—most of them working-class families. The surrounding buildings were Victorians or houses with histories as different as that of the Pearl Apartments.

In the early days of the store, my brother would spend weekends sorting out all the different soda and beer bottles (which also had deposits in those days). However, in his spare time, he would join the neighborhood children and build soapbox racers out of wooden crates from the store and parts cannibalized from roller skates. Once built, they would use the Eddy Street hill as their race course, rattling down the sidewalk.

My brother was almost ten when I was born in 1948 on Flag Day, June 14—three days before my mother's birthday. In order to make him feel part of what was happening, my parents let him name me and he chose Laurence. It was only years later that I found out the reason why. He named me after a saint he had been studying in school—a saint that had died a particularly gruesome death by being roasted on a grill like a leg of lamb. (In fact, he is supposed to have joked to his executioners that they could turn him over because he was done on one side.)

There was never any question of revenge anyway. When your only sibling is ten years older than you are, there isn't the usual rivalry. There is only a long-term sense of inadequacy—and that sense of inadequacy only increased with each year.

One Christmas Day is a kind of white blur because I was dodging Ping-Pong balls all day long whenever my parents were not around. My brother had gotten a gun that resembled a bazooka and had a heavy steel spring and a kind of piston which shot a magazine of Ping-Pong balls. My brother said I resembled a duck in a shooting gallery because as soon as I was hit, I'd turn and try to run in the other direction. In Spike's defense, I should say that I was pretty bratty so I probably had it coming.

Everything climaxed one sunny afternoon when my brother took me and our dog for a walk in the park. In those days, we had a succession of dogs, each named Susie after a girl who used to like to come and help my mother take care of me. Whether the dog was male or female, I insisted on calling it Susie.

It may be that this particular Susie was a boy and resented its name because it made a break for freedom. No sooner did Susie bound away in one direction than I scuttled away in the opposite. Faced with a choice, my brother ran after Susie. He argued, years later, that it was the logical choice because Susie ran faster than I did.

He could always outargue me anyway. He was always the impossible standard by which I tried to measure myself—in sports, in academics, and even in friendship. Spike always seemed to know the right thing to say and do, so that I was always feeling clumsy and inept.

Comparing myself to my athletic father, mother, and brother, I often felt like a changeling, wondering how I wound up being born into the family. I felt not only inadequate but incomplete—like a puzzle with several key pieces missing.

2

LA CONQUISTA

THE ONE thing that ruled my family's lives was our grocery store. I can still smell it. Even today, if I smell old plaster, I feel almost as if I am back in our old storeroom where the plaster was crumbling off the wooden laths. Or if I smell the coppery odor of liver, I think of washing out the bloody porcelain pan in which we used to display that kind of meat. If I smell old dollar bills, I can imagine myself back in the dark, quiet store, helping my mother put away the day's receipts.

A small grocery store is like a big beast that must be continually fed and cared for. Cans, packages, and bottles have to be put on shelves to take the place of things sold, produce like greens and celery have to be nursed along to keep them fresh as long as possible, and there are hundreds of other details that the customers never notice—unless they aren't done. In a small, family-owned store, certain chores must be done at a specific time each day. There is no choice.

Our store had its own daily rhythms just like a farm would have. It began before eight in the morning when my mother would pick her way down the unlit backstairs and along the dark alleyway to the backdoor of the store. Balancing the box with the cash register money in the crook of her arm, she would find the keyhole by feel and let herself in. Then, going through the darkened store, she would put the money in the cash register drawer. There were no neat rolls of coins. Instead, she had them each in a small paper bag, from pennies to fifty-cent pieces, and also dollar bills and bigger denominations in separate sacks.

At about the same time, my father stumped down the front steps of the Pearl Apartments. He usually wore thick-soled shoes for his feet, tan work pants, a flannel shirt, and a felt hat. Though a former athlete, his legs were slowly going bad from having to stand on them constantly for over twelve hours seven days a week. He obviously was carrying no money so there would be no temptation to rob him.

With a little luck, the morning papers were still bundled together meaning that no one had stolen anything. Moving them aside, he would open the wooden door, then the glass door, remove and turn off the homemade burglar alarm, and turn on the lights. Together, my parents did the hundreds of little details necessary to get the store ready for the day at the same time that they would be waiting on customers in a hurry to get to work or school. All day long, trucks would constantly pull into the bus zone outside to make deliveries, which would have to be checked and then put away.

Of all the jobs that had to be done, the one chore my father tried to avoid was cutting up chickens. But he made an exception for one customer. Her husband had taken a kitchen knife and attacked her in front of her children and then tossed her out of the window. Her husband was put in jail, but she was naturally afraid of knives or anything with a sharp edge. My father was always willing to slice up her chickens.

At noontime, there was always a rush of people. Schoolkids out for lunch liked to buy the big dill pickles floating in a jar on the counter. For five cents, a customer could pick out one and my father would reach in with chopsticks to take it out. As fussy as hens, the customers would try to select the largest and my father would fish out their choice with a pair of chopsticks which were slimmer and more practical for maneuvering among the pickles than tongs; but it was an operation that our customers often watched with fascination. Some of the kids also bought a five-cent package of Kool-Aid into which they would dip the pickle itself, alternating bites and dips.

The strangest of all were some of the pregnant women who came into the store. On television it's always something like pickles and ice cream that pregnant women crave. However, these women would hanker for Argo cornstarch and eat it by the lump right in the store.

On and on my parents' day would go until late in the evening when my father would turn off the lights while my mother hid in the back. Turning on our homemade burglar alarm, my father would lock the doors and go home while my mother would sneak out and empty the day's receipts back into the paper sacks and find her way once again up the dark steps in the rear. Even then, their work didn't end since there were account books to be kept; and when they had first bought the store and there was very little money, my father had to figure out each night what stock he could buy for the next day. (However, by the time I was born, the store was on steadier ground.)

My chief job was feeding the beast. Salt pork had to be stacked in the meat counter, mustard greens had to be put out with the other vegetables, boxes of instant grits had to be stacked. The most repetitious and hardest job was putting soda, beer, and wine each day into the big, glass-doored refrigerator we called the icebox. The top of the icebox was decorated with a moving electric waterfall that was an advertisement for a beer company. The cold bottles and cans had to be taken out first and the warm ones put into the back. On election day, butcher paper had to be hung over the door of the beer and wine section because it was illegal to sell liquor that day. The government understandably wanted sober people to vote.

There was stock to be put out on shelves that had been partly adapted from the days when the store had been a *taqueria*. At the base of the shelves on the western wall were bins. In those, we put cans of soup, laying them in rows on their sides. I got fairly good at juggling them, tossing one marked can from my right hand to my left. As my left hand put the can on the shelf, my right hand would already be reaching for the next. (Years later, I tried to learn how to really juggle but couldn't get the knack until my niece made some beanbags in the shape of cans.)

On the other hand, it was always fun to put out the penny bubble gum because it came in boxes with premiums—from china plates to lamps and even TV trays (which came in long, flat boxes with the gum surrounding the items like packing material).

The most fun were the old comic books which we sold for five cents each or six for twenty-five. It was all quite illegal; only we didn't realize it until later. Instead of shipping back old comics that nobody wanted, the magazine distributors would simply tear off the covers of the comics they didn't sell and send them to the publishers to receive credit. However, they still had the coverless comics which they then sold to a man who would put yellow cellophane on as a new kind of cover and sell them to us in bundles.

Cereal, though, was the most challenging item to unpack and sell. It was at the very top of the highest shelves. If a customer wanted a box of Wheaties, for instance, one of us would have to get a pole with a hook at one end. Holding the pole in one hand, we would knock it off the stack and catch it—usually—in the other hand.

Putting up the cereal was even more challenging. My father used it as an opportunity to practice my basketball set shot. As he stood balanced on top of a rickety ladder, I would throw it up in a high rainbow arc so he could catch it. I found the best cereal for throwing was Quaker Oats since it came in a cardboard cylinder.

However, this wasn't as much fun as it sounded because my father would stretch to catch every cereal box. If my shot strayed too wide, I was afraid that my father might reach too far and fall from the ladder. At the very least, I might damage the box and have to finish whatever was inside.

When I was older, I also had to figure out the price of our stock. We belonged to a cooperative of small, independent grocers who, because they bought in large quantities, purchased their groceries cheaply at wholesale prices. The difference between the cost and the selling price was our profit—which in some cases was only pennies; and the prices were listed in a pink book. I would have to multiply that price by a percentage, round it off, and mark the retail price with a special black grease pencil.

After the stock was put up, my job wasn't finished because I would then have to tear up all the cardboard boxes, ripping the flaps so that the boxes could be folded flat, tied up together, and taken out to the garbage cans in the back.

Though they weren't supposed to, the garbagemen would take the piles of cardboard away. In exchange, we said nothing when they helped themselves to bottles of soda that we kept out in the back under the stairs. They, in turn, would sing snatches of opera to one another as they sipped the sodas. Since they came for the garbage sometimes before sunrise, their musical efforts were not always appreciated—they may even be at the root of my dislike of opera today.

There were other chores to be done as well. When we were closing up the store, the fresh vegetables were put into pans of water in the alleyway behind the store and the liver and other meat pans had to be washed out. During the day itself, the soda bottles had to be sorted out; and the related chore I hated most was killing the cockroaches occupying some of the empties. Holding the bottles gingerly, I would take them out to a big zinc tub of water in my father's garden and drown them. Sometimes I also had to help defrost the two freezers, one for vegetables and the other for ice cream. This meant taking a screw driver and a hammer and carefully breaking off the ice without piercing the thin metal pipes that carried the freezing fluid. By the time I had finished dumping all the chunks of ice into a bucket, my fingers would have gone from a painful, aching sensation into a kind of numbness.

There were also nice things about having our own store. If we felt like a midnight snack, we could always make our way down the back stairs and cut ourselves some fresh slices of salami. And it was always easy completing a collection of bubble gum cards because I could go through an entire box and take the extras. Then I would put the proper number back into the pack and reglue the paper again.

Whenever I started to resent my chores, I had my parents' example to make me feel ashamed. My parents merely worked a twelve-hour day, seven days a week, opening for only a half day on Christmas. Later, my father began taking Christmas Day off itself; and eventually even took Sundays off.

Before I was old enough for school and in the summertime, my mother would get away from the store by taking me out in the afternoon before the schoolkids got out and when business was slow.

My parents had bought a used brown '39 Chevy that they renamed Jezebel. Being elderly for a car, Jezebel disliked hills and would protest by wheezing constantly up the slope like an old asthmatic. My mother was known to pat the dashboard with one hand and encourage Jezebel during those efforts.

It was Jezebel who took us out on those afternoon trips. We sometimes went to the petting zoo in the children's part of Golden Gate Park where they had slides, jungle gyms, pony rides, and a wonderful merry-go-round. The little petting zoo had goats, rabbits, and chickens in a miniature barnyard kind of setting. Other times we would go to the real zoo or to the aquarium or to the De Young Museum, which in those days had a marvelous collection of weapons, from small little tankettes from World War I to strange spears with three twisting corkscrewlike blades. My mother accomplished these trips by her own roundabout routes which avoided all left turns and all hills—both of which my mother hated as much as Jezebel did. If you've ever been to San Francisco and seen all of its hills, you'll realize what an achievement this was.

My favorite place, though, was Ocean Beach where I liked to build sand castles and go wading as deep as I could. My mother would roll my pants up my legs and tell me I could only go out to the point where the pants started to get wet. Of course, when she wasn't looking, I would roll the cuffs up even higher until not only my pants but my shirt was soaked.

Just behind the beach were other sights. For years, San Francisco had a small boat, the *Gjoa*, on display that was supposed to have belonged to Roald Amundsen, the first man to reach the South Pole. However, such history lessons failed to impress me as much as the amusement park, Playland at the Beach.

The rides were pretty tame by modern standards—which is why I think the amusement park eventually went under. However, it was fun to go down in the diving bell and come bobbing back up and to play in the fun house which was presided over by a bowing, guffawing dummy known as Laughing Sal.

Of course, there was food, too, including fresh, hot apple turnovers; a kind of caramel popcorn aptly named Yum Yum; and bland enchiladas called bull pups.

At various other times in the neighborhood, there was also a roller skating rink, a miniature golf course, and a place where one could rent and race miniature cars.

Even further up the way near Seal Rock was an ice skating rink that had once held seven pools for bathing. Coupled with the ice skating rink was part of P.T. Barnum's exhibits including hundreds of Egyptian mummies.

However, far more important to me than the physical trips we took through San Francisco were the trips we took in my mind. One of Jezebel's special attractions was her running board. A running board was a kind of step cars used to have beneath the doors. Jezebel's running board provided a perfect springboard for my imagination. In its time, the stationary Jezebel had served as a stagecoach, PT boat, rocket ship, and whatever other vehicle had been required in my games. Shortly after we put new tires on Jezebel, she was stolen—although there were far newer and nicer cars on the block.

My mother and Jezebel had helped out the nuns who ran my school, taking them to the doctor and helping them with other errands. I think the good sisters were almost as distressed as we were so that my teacher actually led the class in prayers to St. Anthony and St. Mary for the return of Jezebel. Despite the efforts of the nuns, we never did get her back. Losing Jezebel was one of the great sorrows of my childhood. Fortunately at the time, my parents never told me what might have happened to her—that she had probably been stripped for her new tires and other parts. It would have been like hearing your pet puppy had been sent to the butcher.

When I was small, I never gave a thought to what my father did while my mother and I were out in Jezebel. He was, of course, back at the store working hard as usual. Eventually the years of heavy lifting and long hours of standing as he waited on customers ruined my father's legs. My parents had put down wooden planks behind the counter over the concrete to try to keep their feet off the cold, hard surface; but even that didn't help my father. The veins in his legs began to swell; but in his tough-minded manner, he simply wound ace bandages around his legs. However, one night when he was changing the bandages, the thin-walled veins tore. Blood came pouring out over the living room before he managed to apply a tourniquet. Though my father had put it off as long as he could, he would have to have an operation on his legs.

Though the operation was successful, my father got himself into trouble almost immediately afterward. Wanting another pillow, he rang for the nurse; but she did not come right away. Even though he was not supposed to stand so soon after his operation, he got out of bed, stumbled to the closet, and got what he wanted. As luck would have it, the nurse finally came in at that moment. The resulting argument eventually led to my father being released early—with both sides being grateful.

Because of the operation though, there were fewer arteries and veins to carry blood through my father's legs. As a result, his legs got cold easily and his leg muscles would start cramping up. It was a painful, awkward condition which he bore in his typical, uncomplaining fashion.

So I hated the store as much as I loved it. It had destroyed my father's legs; and the work itself was boring, repetitious, and physically hard. On the other hand, having a daily routine served me well later when I became a writer. My chores were more than a list of jobs to be done. They gave a rhythm to my day to which I became accustomed—a habit which still proves useful.

Writing a novel is a long process—like a long-distance runner running a marathon. I know that I cannot reach the finish line that day. Instead, I have to be patient, trying to complete a shorter stretch of writing—a chapter, for instance. I can only have faith that I will reach the end; and that belief keeps me plugging away for months to years to finish a draft of a novel— and a novel usually takes several drafts.

Like an old workhorse, I'm most comfortable when I'm in harness: when my days are shaped by a certain routine— though the work is now more mental than physical. I try to write from four to six hours a day plus two more hours of note-taking and reading. Of course, like anyone else, I'm tempted to go outside and enjoy San Francisco when it is sunny outside; and unlike most people I have no boss to keep me at work—or rather I have the hardest of bosses—myself; and so there is a voice inside me still that makes me stay at the computer.

However, La Conquista also gave me more tangible help as a writer. Writers can never tell from where the next idea for a story might come. An idea for a novel might come from the oddest, simplest little thing—provided the writer has some strong feelings for the object. For instance, every now and then in the store we would get old coins including Indian head pennies which my father would give to me. One day we got an odd, yellowish-sort of Indian head penny. My father accepted it even though he thought it might be some sort of counterfeit; but it turned out to be good. Because of a shortage in metals during the Civil War, the 1864 pennies had been made of bronze rather than copper. I kept the penny as a curiosity piece rather than because it had any real value.

Years later, when doing research on San Francisco, I read Edgar Branch's book about Mark Twain when he had been a reporter in San Francisco during the summer of 1864. There were a lot of interesting things about that year both for San Francisco and for Mark Twain since this was right before he wrote "The Celebrated Jumping Frog of Calaveras County," the story that launched his writing career. I was used to think-ing of him as a white-haired genius; but in fact in his younger years he had failed at almost everything he had tried and was about to be fired. By his own admission, he contemplated suicide. Among other stories he covered for his newspaper that summer was a panic in the city because people were afraid that the Confederates would attack San Francisco and loot the gold from the mint. (In my research, I found that there was such a plan but it could not be carried out before the war's end.)

Things began to click. I brought out the penny again and put it on my desk and eventually wrote the books that became *The Mark Twain Murders* and *The Tom Sawyer Fires*.

I don't know, though, if I would have become a writer if my life had been allowed to follow a conventional, comfortable track. However, when I was seven, there was a major change in our lives. The federal government decided to build some low-income housing in our neighborhood. The bureaucrats in that period liked to build huge eleven- and twelve-story monstrosities instead of small units of three stories. The bulldozers and wrecking balls came in and almost overnight demolished most of our friends' houses. In a matter of months, my old world was shattered as I watched the gray lifeless hills rise up over the streets.

Most of the neighborhood had been torn down with the building of the projects; and though some of our old friends and customers stayed on, most of our original neighbors moved away—and with them went our old community and the old network of relationships that my father had used.

In a brief period of time, I lost all of my old friends when their families left; and there was no one to take their place while the old buildings were torn down and the projects were put up. Too young to go into Chinatown by myself, I felt myself isolated and alone within the ruins of my old neighborhood. As tractors roared across the street, I puzzled over what had happened. Had I done something wrong? Was this a punishment? I wound up falling back upon my own imagination, learning to value games that I could play by myself.

In the space of two years, the neighborhood became mostly

black. Although we missed our old neighbors, most of our new neighbors were just trying to survive; and though my father was a gruff man, he had a soft spot for young families who were trying to make it—perhaps remembering his own early days. Even though we had a sign saying not to ask for credit, he carried quite a few of our new customers. Their signed receipts were kept on a spike next to the roll of butcher paper behind the counter. Even when some of these customers moved out of the projects, they remembered us. Each month, one family would come and do their heavy shopping at our store because we had helped them through some difficulties. Then, too, since we had been there before most of the people moved into the projects, we were a fixture of the neighborhood.

Another Chinese by the name of Harvey decided to take advantage of all those new customers by building a new grocery store a block to the west up the Eddy Street hill.

The other little grocery stores in the area were also owned by Chinese. A block to the north was the Good Fortune owned by a man called Cal who belonged to the same grocers' cooperative as us. However, when the unions went on strike against the wholesale association, they put up a picket line around his store. Cal let them picket him for the morning but for the afternoon, in the spirit of fairness, he decided that he ought to share his company with us so he informed the pickets that we also belonged to the same association and charitably sent them down to us.

Harvey, though, was something else. The very first day he opened, he took off his smock, came down to our store, inspected the prices on various items, and then went back up the hill to mark his prices below ours.

One Christmas Day when my father finally began to take the day off for the holiday, we found we didn't have any batteries for a new toy that my oldest niece, Franny, received. Since there were no batteries in our store, it was necessary to go up the hill and buy some from our rival. I can't remember how we decided who should go, but it wound up being me, much to my great embarrassment at the time. I trudged into the store, wishing I could wear a bag over my head, and bought the batteries without saying a word by simply pointing and giving them the money. I wasn't about to speak to the enemy.

Harvey's style of store management differed greatly from my father's. When my father caught someone shoplifting, he usually gave them a scolding or talked to their friends and family. But Harvey would grab a broom and would give chase to the thief, pursuing him or her even into the projects and up and down the hallways and stairs.

Unfortunately, the projects had been built in such a way that it was impossible to tell who lived there and who was a stranger bent on some mischief, so it was easy to hide there. As things got rougher, Cal and Harvey installed fancy burglar alarms in their stores; but the burglars knew they lived elsewhere and that the police would take their time to respond. At about two or three in the morning, the thieves would smash a store window so that the jangling alarm would wake the entire neighborhood. The thieves would then take what they wanted; the cop car would eventually roll up, call Cal or Harvey, and then wait. In the meantime, however, the alarm kept the neighborhood up until the appropriate owner finally arrived to turn it off and tell the police what was missing.

In general, we never had the problems that Harvey and Cal had because we got on with most of the neighbors. And those who were capable of theft knew that we lived above the store so that burglary wasn't practical.

But occasionally some stranger from outside our neighborhood would also try to break into our store. My father, though, had rigged up his own homemade burglar alarm. Since my bedroom was over the store, near the door where the alarm was, I was the first to hear an attempted break-in. To this day,

I can't hear an alarm clock without feeling my stomach tensing and experiencing all the other reactions I used to go through with the burglar alarm. My wife, Joanne, cannot understand how I can become more or less alert in a manner of seconds; but it's conditioning from the burglar alarm. Fortunately, with all the lights going on in our second-floor apartment and all the shouting, every burglar scooted off.

I knew my father had begun to worry when he took one of the toy bats I had used when I was five—a small wooden one—and he began to wrap cord around the bat grip so he could hold it better. He then kept the modified toy in the storeroom as a weapon. He never used it. I don't think he was capable of swinging it to hurt someone; but it helped his peace of mind to have something like that for an emergency. Other Chinese grocers began to keep guns.

Eventually one night a gang of junior high boys came into the neighborhood looking for some fun (as some of our neighbors later found out and told my father). Wanting to impress the girls who were with them, they tried to get some wine from our store windows.

The burglar alarm was hooked up to the door—the normal point of entry for the burglars. However, one of the boys tied a rag around his hand and began to break the window. We might not have noticed it later at night; but this was around ten when everyone was still up. My father charged down the steps and I followed.

In their inexperience, the boys lingered on and so my father caught the would-be burglar. He yelled up to my mother to call the police and then, as the gang closed in, my father kept his arm locked around the boy's throat. With our backs to the wall, we kept the boy as a shield between us and the rest of the gang.

The minutes ticked by like hours. Where were the police? The gang members frantically blustered and threatened. Fortunately, they had no weapons of their own; but they claimed our prisoner had an older brother who did have a gun and who would get even with us if we didn't let the boy go. I still remember the faces lit by the street light; and I can still remember the fear knotting my stomach while I stood with my father against the wall.

After about ten agonizing minutes, the boy broke free and the whole gang ran off. My father chased them to the corner and just stood there in frustration cursing with words I had never heard him use before. After another ten minutes, a patrol car rolled up. A very bored policeman took the report that we knew would be dumped into the circular file.

Looking back, it was just as well the boys got away. No self-respecting judge would put a boy in juvenile hall for a broken window, even a large store window; and what if the boys' threats had been true? What if there had been an older brother with a gun who would get even? For years after this confrontation, I became uncomfortable in a crowd; and I still don't like being among large numbers of people.

The next day, my father got a hammer and began smashing the rest of the glass out of the window. His face full of fury and exasperation, he swung the hammer each time with all of his strength. Then we went and got sheets of plywood, sawed it, set it up in place, and painted it—all before the end of the day. No more gangs would be able to break in through the windows; but it turned our store into a dark, gloomy cave.

3

THE
NEIGHBORHOOD

WHEN MARK TWAIN was young, he worked on the large steamboats that traveled up and down the Mississippi River. He once said that he learned everything he needed to know about human nature on board those ships.

In a way, the grocery store was my version of one of Mark Twain's steamboats, giving me my first schooling as a writer. I saw people at their best; and I saw them at their worst. I saw people in the middle of comedies; and, sadly, I saw them in the middle of tragedies into which we were drawn in minor roles. Often we were like actors who had wandered onto a stage without a script so that we had to improvise as best we could. As a result, we all became good listeners.

I suppose if I hadn't become a writer, I might have followed the strategy of one of our truck drivers. He had been a monk in a monastery but had taken a leave to see what the rest of the world was like. After driving his route in our neighborhood for a few months, he said he would be glad to return to the monastery.

Though perhaps I could not have put it into those exact words, I think I realized at an early age that what made people most interesting were their imperfections. Their quirks were what made them unique and set them apart from everyone else. As a writer nowadays, I know that a character can come to life in a sentence if I can give him or her a "quirk"—whether it's the way they look or dress, some habitual gesture, or some favorite phrase—that makes them special.

Jimmy was an Italian truck driver who delivered beer to our store. He referred to anyone who was an idiot as a salami and in his judgment most of the world was populated by cold cuts. In fact, when his association put up a statue of Columbus, he went into a whole smorgasbord of insults. There had been a heated discussion about what direction Columbus should face—eastward in the direction of the Caribbean Islands he had found or westward in the direction he had been sailing until those islands got in the way. In any event, Jimmy felt they had chosen the wrong direction. There was enough salami flung that day to outfit a deli.

We had one middle-aged customer who liked to dress himself in the fashions he wore back when he was young. As a result, he would put on something called a zoot suit which had shoulders broad enough for a linebacker. At night, he would go out on the town, dressed to kill. He would always come back drunk and one time, he had gone out in all of his splendor on a rainy day. While he was away, the sewer backed up, flooding the intersection outside our store. As he staggered home after an evening in the bar, he fell into the water. Thinking he had fallen into the San Francisco Bay, he kept floundering and calling for help until my father pulled him out. His gratitude was immense that day and so was his embarrassment the next.

Another interesting customer painted houses. Later, when he was trying to start his own contracting business, we let him paint our house. However, unknown to us, he was using non-union labor so we immediately had picket signs around us. Worse, he could not afford to buy his paint all at one time. Instead, he only had enough paint to cover one side of the house with the shade of green that my mother had selected. However, when he went back to buy more paint, the company could not match the original color. As a result, we wound up with a two-tone house, with one side a darker green than the other. My father eventually became philosophical about it, deciding that it was sufficient if our two-toned building became a single color at least for a few hours each day. In the late afternoon, the long shadows would fall on the lighter side of our building so that it would finally match the darker side.

Above all, I remember the kindness of customers like Mr. Woodrow who was the favorite audience for my oldest niece, Franny. She used to help in the store, and each day she saw Mr. Woodrow she would tell him the same joke about Abraham Lincoln and his wife, and each day he would laugh uproariously. (The irony, of course, is that nowadays she can remember most of the joke except for the punchline.)

However, working in the store taught me not only about our customers but about myself as well. Almost as soon as I knew how to make change, I also helped wait on customers during busy times—and received one of my first lessons in etiquette: Someone's poverty was no excuse for bad manners.

Once when an elderly customer made a small purchase, I handed him his change and his purchase in a sack and repeated a phrase I sometimes heard my mother and father use. "Thank you," I said. "Come again." However, it was one of those days when I didn't want to work in the store—to be honest, there weren't many days I wanted to work in the store—so I said the phrase in a bored way.

He gave a curt nod of his head. "I will, sonny, soon's I get some more money."

I recall everyone in the store laughing except for the old man and me. I learned that day not to use polite phrases unless I meant it. Beyond that, it taught me that just because a person lacks money doesn't mean that he or she also lacks dignity.

Because of the people I met in our store, I came to have little patience with stories about rich and wealthy people. Even before I began selling what I wrote, I was trying to tell stories about characters who survive at a basic level; and now when I look for folktales to tell, I usually look for stories about ordinary people rather than about princes and princesses.

On the other side of the coin, I also learned not to trust too many people no matter how harmless they looked. On another occasion, I waited on a little girl who was small with a broad grin and who seemed pleasant and even innocent enough.

She pointed to a Hershey's candy bar and put a nickel on the counter. I took the coin, put it on the cash register, and bent down to get the candy bar from behind the counter. When I gave it to her, she asked for another. Taking her money, I put it on the cash register again and got another candy bar. When she repeated this a couple of more times, I began to grow impatient, wondering why she couldn't make up her mind and buy them all at once; but I kept bending over and getting her selection from underneath the counter.

Finally, though, my father caught her. Everytime I had bent to get a new candy bar, she had been taking the same nickel from the little wooden ledge above the cash register. My father let her keep the candy she had conned out of me but told her to get out. He didn't scold me; he just gave me one of those stern, sad looks that were more effective than scoldings.

A silent, enigmatic witness to my downfall was Saul the Junkman. He was one part mentor, one part watch dog, and the third part was kept secret from everyone. He used to sit on a spare roll of butcher paper that he turned on one end and used as a stool in front of the potato chip rack. In the early days of the store, he and my father had been partners in some enterprise. They weren't partners any longer legally or professionally; but spiritually once you had been Saul's partner, you were his partner for life.

Once seated he would smoke his cheap cigars, which he paid for by returning shopping carts to a supermarket that had opened up a few blocks away. (Sometimes he would get into a tug-of-war with the neighborhood children who were also trying to claim the cart as theirs.) The stench from his cigars was so awful that my parents kept a small electric fan on the counter to blow the smoke away from them; and they would turn it on even on cold winter nights. I don't think he even noticed, for he would sit staring up meditatively as the smoke wreathed about his head.

He had come from Poland and served in the army during World War I. Once he took my toy rifle and smartly showed me the manual of arms which are the maneuvers a soldier does with a rifle. He had also wrestled professionally for a while before settling down in the junk business. Across the street and down half a block was an old gray stable that had been converted by a practical-minded landlord who had poured cement down on the floor. He kept his truck and some of his treasures there, living elsewhere.

When someone needed to clean out an attic or a basement, they would call Saul; and he would chug out in his old green Ford truck. It had been built in the 1920s so that the driver's compartment was more or less open. On sunny days, it was like riding around in a convertible except that we rode high off the street like a pair of kings; and stopping was even more exciting—especially if it was on a hill because Saul's brakes were uncertain. While he tried to curb his wheels, whoever his passenger was would jump out and try to place wooden blocks under the tires.

When and if the truck stopped, the job was more like a regular treasure hunt than work. There was no telling what might be housed in the dusty old boxes he hauled out of the houses: stuffed squirrels, old phonograph records, wooden legs. Some of it he would sell to the antique dealers a few blocks away, other things he would sell himself. Riding with Saul was always an adventure with treasures at the end.

On general principle, Saul hated for anything to go to waste. Perhaps we would call him a recycler now. He would claim the violet tissue that protected our apples in the crates and use it as his facial tissue. However, when he ran out of apple wrappers, he would simply stand on the back stairs, lean over, and use his fingers without any warning or checking to see who was below. I soon learned to recognize his distinctive shuffle overhead so I could stay under the protection of the stairs.

Saul's other passion beside cigars was wrestling. At the old Winterland, a few blocks away, they used to put on wrestling matches. I was too small, but my brother would accompany Saul. He would return, his face flushed from shouting and his clothes reeking of the cheap cigars smoked in the arena.

More importantly, Saul was my companion and bodyguard at Halloween when it was my job to pass out the candy from a big hundred-pound rice can. My mother had filled it with penny candy, tootsie rolls, and little squares of candy wrapped in wax paper called Kits.

Sometimes the number of trick-or-treaters could be quite large; and I suppose I might have been overwhelmed if it had not been for Saul. It was a rough neighborhood after all: One of the pastimes among the older, more enterprising children was to go down to Fillmore Street and wait for a drunk to stagger out of a bar. Shouting trick-or-treat, they would surround him. Without candy, the drunk might give them some money; and there was always the chance that the drunk would mistake a ten-dollar bill for a one. Saul, though, was usually there for the crush. If he thought a child had been there before, he would dip his hand into the bright red, hundred-pound rice can and bring up a fist filled with candy. Thrusting his arm into the child's bag, he would rap the side so that it would sound and feel as if candy were dropping in. In reality, he never opened his fingers. He was quite proud of the trick and tried to teach it to me. However, feeling guilty, I would pretend to be clumsy—something I was good at. Some of the children he thought were cheats I was sure had not been there before. (This makes Saul sound mean; but he was also capable of taking the time to sit down with a boy who was having trouble in school and teaching him to read.)

Dressed in an old felt hat, gray coat sweaters, and tan work pants, Saul was probably the last person you would pick to be a lover of beauty. However, in all his years of hauling trash, he would keep the cut glass—vases, tumblers, goblets, and other objects. I think there was something about the way they caught the light because he had displayed some of his collection in a big sideboard with mirrors in back that could help reflect the light through them.

After Jezebel was stolen, we rented a converted stable next to Saul's; and in it we kept Jezebel's successor, a yellow Mercury. The "Merc" was a heavy car that probably only got five miles to the gallon; but it was once broadsided by a bus and sent rolling across Geary Boulevard. Not only did we survive the accident, but the mechanics up the street, the Ferreiras,* repaired the dents so that the Merc could go on chugging slow and steady as a tank. (There are not too many cars nowadays that could survive a collision with a city bus.)

When they first bought the store, my parents made friends

---

*Later, they specialized in repairing old cars and one of their automobiles was featured in the film *Tucker*.

with other young couples who had children the same age as my brother. My mother went out to shows with the other wives while my father and the husbands babysat the children. It was with their children that in his spare time my brother built soapbox racers; and it was also with them that he went hunting and fishing.

When my parents bought one of the first televisions, it was quite an event in the neighborhood. The television screen wasn't more than nine inches diagonally; but it was housed in a massive cabinet with a wood veneer that also held a phonograph player—so I suppose it would be called a home entertainment center nowadays.

The first night, my father and brother brought up planks and milk cartons to create bleachers; and my mother boiled dozens of hot dogs. Then we invited the whole neighborhood in to see the electronic wonder. Adults and children watched the same shows from *Howdy Doody* to midget wrestling. However, the group wasn't always passive. There were also huge group picnics down at a park in San Mateo with softball games and other activities.

The biggest, most important group event, though, was in the fall when we would go see 49er games. In those days the team played in Kezar Stadium, a small place which had been built for high school football games. Since the stadium was only a mile and a half away, it was in easy walking distance. So, loaded down with hot dogs, a big thermos of Kool-Aid, and blankets and cushions for the splintery wooden benches, the group would hike up to the stadium, pay a few dollars for tickets in the end zone, watch the game, and then return home talking about the passing of Frankie Albert and the running of Joe "the Jet" Perry.

(I still have Joe Perry's autograph; but the autograph I treasure the most is Leo "the Lion" Nomellini who played on both the offensive and defensive lines. He subsequently turned professional wrestler and often wrestled—performed would probably be a better word—at Winterland.)

Down the block on Eddy Street was Mr. Vincent, the mortician. Most of the children and even some of the adults shied away from him; but he was fond of telling them that his customers never hurt anyone. It was the live ones you had to watch out for. When he was in the right mood, I could usually get him to "talk shop" about the grislier aspects of his work.

Almost as interesting a set of conversationalists as Mr. Vincent were another group of neighbors who were among the few whites living in the neighborhood. Because the rents were so cheap in the area, we had a group of white filmmakers next door. In those days, they would have been called beatniks. One of them was a tall, bald man with one gold earring in his ear—which was still a fascinating fashion accessory for a man in those days and intrigued the whole neighborhood. A gentle giant, he was always smiling so the neighborhood children took to calling him Mr. Clean, after the character in a set of advertisements running on television at the time. He would stroll up the street with a troop of boys and girls trailing him as if he were some bald, smiling pied piper. He and his friends filmed epics in their living room, including, they said, their own version of *Ben Hur*.

As time went on, though, things got rougher. The gangs that drifted in were older, tougher, and more dangerous. If we were lucky, they only came in to shoplift Twinkies and cupcakes and other junk food. If there was enough of them, they stripped the shelves openly. There was no point in calling the police. Assuming that they eventually showed up and assuming that they caught the shoplifters, there was no judge who would sentence them to youth detention for stealing snacks; and yet it was our livelihood that was being slowly bled away.

By that point, my father had also rigged up his own intercom to our apartment. When my mother was upstairs and the store had suddenly got crowded, he would turn it on and ask her to come down to help. The intercom, though, went on with a funny, high kind of squeal that was audible throughout the store. Once when a group of kids came in to rob my father, he managed to turn on the intercom first. The loud squeal startled them. Perhaps they thought it was the police, or perhaps they thought it was some new, exotic alarm. At any rate, they ran out of the store.

The troubles we had, though, were nothing compared to the other grocers. When Cal grew tired of broken windows at the Good Fortune, he tried to replace the glass with plywood as my father had done with our store. However, Cal's precautions didn't discourage one set of burglars who simply stole a car and backed it up across the sidewalk and smashed through the plywood-covered windows. Driving the car forward, they then went through the gaping, splintery hole and took what they wanted.

Eventually the other grocers began to pack guns. My father, however, refused to go that far; and in fact, we were never robbed of cash in all the years we had the store. Toward the end, gangs would come in and openly take whatever they wanted; but they never actually tried to get into the cash register.

By that time, a new community had developed in our neighborhood and so I felt like an outsider in what had once been my own home turf. With the building of the projects, most of my original friends had moved away. Though I knew a wide number of neighborhood boys and girls, the acquaintanceship was through the store. If I wanted to play basketball or football, I went into Chinatown to play with my schoolmates.

In my own neighborhood, I can remember one time when I was helping to bring in a shipment from our wholesaler. The big semitrailer would pull into the bus stop outside the store and the boxes would be stacked up in columns. Once we had checked the count and signed for it, we would wheel in the boxes with a hand truck. (For someone young like my niece, Franny, my father could make quite a game of it by having the child get on the hand truck and wheeling her through the store, calling out various funny-sounding train stops like Cucamonga.)

However, while the groceries were being brought inside, someone had to watch the ones on the sidewalk. I remember a group of children who came down the block, both black and white. They were pretending they were soldiers in World War II. Suddenly they began making me a target, assuming that I was Japanese.

Saul came along and chased them off; but I realized that I was the neighborhood's all-purpose Asian. I could have also been the Korean- or Chinese-Communist who got killed, depending upon what war they were pretending to fight. It made me feel like an outsider more than ever in my own neighborhood. It was like suddenly finding that the different pieces of a jigsaw puzzle no longer fit together.

I can't pretend to guess what the other neighborhood children thought of me. However, in general I think we had fewer problems than the other Chinese grocers because our new neighbors watched out for us. There was one man in particular who set himself up as our unofficial guardian angel. Madison was a huge, hulking man who had played tackle on a semipro football team. He worked for a janitorial service; and he filled his uniform coveralls so that they always seemed ready to split. However, all the children in the neighborhood called this mammoth man, Mo-mo. His nieces, unable to say his real name when they were small, had called him that; and the other children had picked it up.

Once, there was a gang of kids studying our store from across the street. Mo-mo overheard them talking about knocking over the place. He stormed right into them and held his fist up to the ringleader. "If you bust Tom's, I'll bust your head." The wide-eyed boys took off; and we never saw them again.

Mo-mo later made it into the local newspapers and became a neighborhood celebrity. Given the number of nude beaches and what gets shown on cable television today, it all seems rather tame now. However, when the topless clubs opened on Broadway, it was still risqué to have a woman display her breasts in public. Of course, the dancers soon found they needed gimmicks. One was the topless mother of eight, another danced on top of a piano that came down from the ceiling. A third woman with a more zoological bent used to perform with a python.

Since the snake was both part of her livelihood and a pet, she took it everywhere in a basket—even when she went shopping. However, one day when she was in a department store, she left the basket on a counter while she went to look at something. Immediately a thief grabbed the basket and ran off. Of course, she was in a panic at losing one half of her act. However, the police recovered the snake and a rather shaken thief.

At any rate, the snake lady was returning home late one morning in a taxicab when another car shot through the intersection and collided with them.

Mo-mo happened to live in an apartment near the intersection. Hearing the crash, he had gotten groggily out of bed to check on his new car that he had parked outside. Still blinking the sleep from his eyes, he went to raise the window—forgetting that the window was already open. He went straight through the open window and fell a full story to the pavement. Fortunately, he was still so sleepy that he didn't have time to realize what was happening and was still very relaxed when he hit the concrete so that he didn't break any bones.

However, the police then had to call for another ambulance besides the one for the snake lady and her snake. Of course,

Mo-mo was still only in his pajamas when they wheeled him into the hospital.

The admitting nurse came over and began to fill out the form. When she asked Mo-mo if he had insurance, he answered, "Yes."

"Would you," the nurse asked, "remember what company it was?"

And Mo-mo said, "It's Blue Cross." And he whipped his insurance card out of his pajamas and handed it to the astonished nurse. Apparently, Mo-mo always went to sleep with his insurance card safely on hand.

Mo-mo, it seemed, was always prepared.

4

THE
OWL

LIKE MANY other Chinese children of the time, I thought of myself as American. I can remember watching an old black-and-white cartoon on television—I think it was about a character called Scrappy. In it, he quarreled with a group of Chinese laundrymen so that he and they got into a comic-pitched battle.

The caricatures with the exaggerated slanted eyes and characters clad in black pajamas seemed fantasy creatures; and I remember putting my fingers up by the sides of my eyes to slant them like the characters in the cartoon and running around making high, sing-song noises. My horrified mother said to me, "You're Chinese. Stop that."

Since that amounted to harsh words for my mother, I slunk off ashamed. Later, I dragged a chair over to the fireplace and climbed up so I could look at myself in the round mirror that hung over the mantle. My mother was right. Though my eyes were not slanted, I had folds at the corners of my eyes that created that effect.

I stopped doing imitations of cartoon laundrymen; but I still didn't particularly want to be Chinese. In my neighborhood, I had grown up thinking that I was as American as all the other children. In the 1950s, few people wanted to be strange and different—let alone foreign.

Nowadays there is a good deal of nostalgia about that time—about Elvis Presley, drive-in restaurants, juke boxes, and gas-eating cars. I grew up then so that I know it wasn't pleasant. I would never care to go back. It was as if everyone in America was in one giant parade; and we were all expected to march in the same direction and at the same pace. Any attempt to change course or slow down brought ridicule and even trampling. There were immense pressures on white children to conform—to be like all the other children in their school and neighborhood instead of themselves; and the pressures were even greater on the minorities to be like the whites.

Besides, to be Chinese in San Francisco simply brought trouble. I can remember taking a walk in Golden Gate Park with a friend. We had brought along our lunches in paper bags and were enjoying the fragrant silence of the eucalyptus trees when some boys—white boys—suddenly came around the bend. They called us various names. At first, it took me a moment to realize they were talking to us; and then I was in such a state of shock that I didn't say anything which, given their numbers, was probably just as well. My friend just ignored them and kept walking. In a daze, I followed. One of our tormentors made hawking noises and spat. It was only later that I looked at my lunch bag and saw that he had connected, so I threw it away and went hungry for the rest of the day.

Just north of Chinatown is the Italian section of San Francisco called North Beach. Because the only stretch of grass in

Chinatown was a small plot of grass behind the Chinatown projects, we would take our football and go up to the large lawns of Washington Square, which sat in the heart of the North Beach section. Once a group of Italian boys tried to chase us out. They had a kind of swagger that was hard to understand at first. By that time, most of us had learned to ignore such fools until they moved on.

However, this time, one of them pulled out a knife—as if it were a new toy. The knife got our notice, of course. There were some long, tense moments while they taunted us; but they were satisfied with kicking our football off into the trees and moved on.

At a time when so many children are now proud of their ethnic heritages, I'm ashamed to say that when I was a child, I didn't want to be Chinese. It took me years to realize that I was Chinese whether I wanted to be or not. And it was something I had to learn to accept: to know its strengths and understand its weaknesses. It's something that is a part of me from the deepest levels of my soul to my most common, everyday actions. For one thing, my wife, Joanne, tells me that my family and I speak to one another in a different rhythm than what we use outside the home, our voices rising and falling though we are speaking English.

Or perhaps I should say I am a Chinese American rather than Chinese because I could never fit in China either. Jeanne Wakatsuki Houston, who wrote *Farewell to Manzanar*, tells a story of going to Japan for the first time and walking up to a guard at the Tokyo airport to ask a question. However, before she could even open her mouth, the guard smiled and said in English, "You are American, no?" Though she might look Japanese, her walk and very posture said differently.

Perhaps I might have felt differently if my family had lived in Chinatown. All my uncles and aunts and cousins still lived in or near Chinatown; and in those days it was much smaller.

I saw them often—our family celebrated every birthday and holiday together—but it wasn't the same as growing up there. It wasn't until 1965 when the immigration laws were changed, making it possible for more Asians to enter the country, that it changed.

Back in the nineteenth century and the early part of the twentieth century, it was difficult if not impossible for a Chinese man to bring his wife over from China. As a result, a Chinese man would work in America for five or more years. Then, if he was lucky, he would get to return to China and stay for a year or so before returning. So, though most of the Chinese were married and had families, they lived most of their lives as bachelors. World War II and then the victories of the Communists made it impossible for them to return home.

So that was the Chinatown that I knew—a place where almost everyone could speak English as well as Chinese. It was small and intimate—both in terms of area and population. At the same time, over the decades, Grant Avenue, the heart of Chinatown, had developed a facade for the tourists.

In those days, America had placed a trade embargo against Mainland China because they supported the non-Communist Chinese government on Taiwan. Because of the embargo, it was impossible for the souvenir stores to get Chinese goods from Mainland China.

However, the stores had to sell something to the white tourists so, outside of a few things from Hong Kong, and a few dusty statues left over from the old days, the stores stocked Japanese goods. They sold geisha dolls and kimonos as souvenirs of Chinatown. (This could sometimes reach absurd lengths. One friend worked for a man who owned souvenir stores in both Japantown and Chinatown so my friend would alternate in the different stores. Both stores sold the same goods. The only difference for my friend was the type of coat he had to wear to wait on the tourists.)

Again, tourists expected to buy certain things in Chinatown that would not have been allowed to be sold in the Woolworth's back at home. Some of them were fairly harmless—like the plastic backscratchers that said on the stem: Souvenir of Chinatown (but in smaller print said, Made in New Jersey). However, the tourists also wanted a variety of signs and souvenirs that ranged from the vulgar to the obscene. And sometimes they were downright dangerous—like the various pellet guns and types of knives.

(In high school, there was one Italian boy who was friendly to the Chinese because he made his spending money by going into Chinatown to buy knives and then selling them to the other Italian kids in the North Beach section who didn't want to travel the six blocks into Chinatown.)

So, in my ignorant way, I also associated being Chinese with the artificial and commercial "Asian-ness" of the windows. Acupuncture, in which needles are used to direct the flow of energy in a body, was weird if not dangerous; herbalism produced awful-smelling concoctions. Even the martial arts like kung fu and tai chi chuan were old-fashioned superstitions. A friend told us almost apologetically that he was studying with one of the masters of Chinatown. At the time, he might just as well have said that he was going to grow his hair in a pigtail— as the old Chinese once had to wear when the Manchus conquered China.

Nor did we Chinese Americans fit in all that well with the old-timers. When my parents had been teenagers, they had been scolded for ruining their stomachs with American soda pop. Worse, as I said, the girls would play basketball with the boys.

However, the old-timers could have their kindly side. Because of World War II and the politics of the times, many of the old-timers had not been able to see their families in years and so there was a kind of general good feeling toward children. As a boy, my brother could go into butcher shops in Chinatown and ask for and get a free piece of *char siu* (barbecued pork). And when I was small and shopped in Chinatown with my mother, I could still get a treat myself.

Nothing, though, really comes for free. There are always strings attached to a gift. The old-timers were kind to us as long as they thought we were Chinese. For a time in our neighborhood, there was an elderly Chinese, Timothy, who rented a building near us where he did laundry. If he thought he could not remove the stains from an item, he would shove it back, saying, "Too dirty, too dirty." Since that was the precise reason why would-be customers wanted it cleaned, they would leave the laundry and come down to us so we could explain what Timothy meant.

Once, my brother and I were driving to Chinatown in the Merc when we saw Timothy waiting at the bus stop. It was impossible to miss him because he was bent forward by years of work. My brother pulled into the bus stop and had me roll down the window to ask Timothy if he needed a lift into Chinatown. He got in readily enough, but then asked us something in Chinese. When we didn't answer right away, he immediately suspected the truth—that we could not speak Chinese. For the rest of the trip, he scolded us in broken English for forgetting that we were Chinese.

In my own neighborhood, I was Tom's son, the boy who worked in a grocery store and lived above it. I knew more or less who I was. But all that meant nothing once the electric streetcar crackled its way through the Stockton tunnel and I entered Chinatown and met with my grandmother.

She represented a "Chineseness" in my life that was as unmovable and unwanted as a mountain in your living room. Or rather it was like finding strange, new pieces to a puzzle that made the picture itself take a new, unwanted shape. In Chinatown, Tom's son became Gim's son, for my father was known by his Chinese name there.

As much as I tried to deny my ethnic background, I was unable to escape completely from being Chinese because of my grandmother, Marie Lee.

The youngest in her family, she had married as a teenager. Her husband was a scholar who had been studying for the government exams that would earn him a government post. The exams, though, did not involve arithmetic or other practical skills but were on the Chinese classics instead. The philosophy behind the exams had been simple: a gentleman-scholar would be equally adept at essay writing and governing. Skill in the former would reflect future skill in the latter. That had been the way for thousands of years; but all that changed in October 1911 when China became a republic.

I've said that my grandmother represented a "Chineseness" to me; but in many ways she, too, was an outsider and not like her other friends in Chinatown. She had lived for quite a while not only outside of Chinatown but miles away from any other Chinese woman. As a result, she had developed a kind of self-reliant toughness. In fact, she was actually an interesting blend of China and the Midwest.

As I mentioned, she followed my grandfather east into the heartland of America and eventually to West Virginia where she and Miss Alcinda hit it off somehow. It was Miss Alcinda who taught my grandmother English so—since my grandfather only spoke Chinese—my grandmother must have been the one to wait on customers.

More importantly, my grandmother learned how to bake apple pies, which were always popular at the church socials. As my grandmother told me, they were always the first to be sold. My mother also remembers her mother making wonderful doughnuts for the church socials—though the children especially loved the doughnut holes.

Though my Auntie Rachel—my mother's youngest sister—remembers the Ku Klux Klan being active in the town, my family seems to have been generally accepted. My mother and my aunts and uncle grew up more or less like their American playmates.

The reasons aren't really too clear for their leaving; but I think one concern of my grandmother was that her children were growing up too wild—meaning American—and she wanted her girls to meet nice Chinese boys. She never budged from California again and rarely emerged even from Chinatown.

My mother tells me that my grandmother dressed stylishly in the twenties; but by the time I knew her, she dressed "sensibly," usually wearing several sweaters and vests over a blouse or pajama top to be covered—when we went out—by a heavy cloth coat. As a result, when I hugged her, it was difficult to tell how much was her and how much was her wardrobe.

She lived in a studio apartment in an alley called Brooklyn Place. At one end of the studio apartment was a tiny shower and toilet; and at the other was a kitchenette into which my grandmother could barely squeeze. Every inch of space in the studio was accounted for. Between the door and the bathroom sat her phonograph player and Chinese records as well as her radio within reach of the bed. On the opposite wall was a cabinet and boxes neatly stacked with most of her possessions. Next to them was a small table with two chairs. On the table itself was a checkerboard cloth and a restaurant napkin dispenser. Finally, on the other side of the kitchen doorway was her bureau with her statues and her gifts for any of her nine grandchildren who might visit—sometimes four silver quarters or other change, sometimes cookies, sometimes comic books.

Her "Chineseness" began with the smell of her studio apartment—a smell that clung even to her clothes when we went outside; and that I noticed on the clothes of some of the older Chinese. It was a mixture of tiger balm, a kind of cure-all salve, and the incense sticks she would burn for the gods and goddesses on top of her bureau.

The incense sticks caused my mother no end of trouble when she tried to buy them for my grandmother. If the company changed the label, my grandmother would suspect that they were a different—and probably inferior—brand.

Since she didn't have enough English and I didn't have enough Chinese, we couldn't talk about such things as the statues on her bureau. On the other hand, the plastic Jesus on our car dashboard was the "pretty lady with the beard." She could no more discuss America with me than I could discuss China with her.

Instead, what I learned, I picked up in a subtle fashion, soaking up things like a sponge so that years later I was able to use it in a book. It happened during those weekly walks with her, down the thirteen steps from her studio to the apartment porch and down the four steps to the sidewalk. She moved slowly but determinedly like the little engine that could, down Brooklyn Place, across busy Sacramento Street and down another alley that now has a sign calling it Hang Ah Alley but that was nameless then as far as I know.

I became fairly good at maneuvering to give her maximum support as she held onto my arm. Often, we would chat about the obstacles on the way—the bumps and cracks becoming almost like old friends in their familiarity.

We would head down Sacramento Street to Waverly Place and down a steeply slanting sidewalk to Uncle's. It was a typical old-timers' place with Formica tables and elderly men in suits almost as old. Sometimes the suits would bag on the wearers as if their bodies had once been bigger—as if the wearer were shrinking with age. Food there was good if simple, plentiful, and cheap. (If you want to pay for food rather than for decor, throw away the tour books and gourmet guides and look in Chinatown for the restaurants where the old-timers and families are eating.)

The waiter in a short-sleeve white shirt and bow tie would bring my grandmother a huge, steaming plate of rice heaped with freshly cooked *bok choy*—a kind of green vegetable that can come in a variety of sizes. My grandmother could be quite fussy about even that simple vegetable, preferring it when it was picked young with little yellow flowers still on the small stalks because it was most tender and juiciest then. At the restaurant, my grandmother would even send it back if she thought the chef had used too much oil. Oil, she liked to sniff, was what sloppy and incompetent cooks used to hide their mistakes.

My mother and I would get our orders, usually a veal cutlet dinner with mashed potatoes. Though my grandmother took Chinese food quite seriously—almost religiously, she had the opposite opinion of American food. One time when my second niece, Lisa, was having lunch with my grandmother, she was delighted to hear that Lisa's two favorite foods were catsup and mashed potatoes. She got a catsup bottle from the waiter and urged Lisa to mix the two together, creating a pink mess that Lisa dutifully ate.

We always topped off the meal with slices of orange custard pie. As if my mother were a little girl again, my grandmother would take a fork and scrape off the whipped cream from her pie and add it to my mother's portion. My mother never protested.

Periodically when we ate at Uncle's, my grandmother would replenish her napkin supply. Waiting until the waiter was out of sight, my grandmother would squeeze her fingers into the napkin dispenser so she could take out napkins by the handful. Treating the napkins as if they were sheaves of government secrets, my grandmother would slip them to my mother underneath the table so my mother could hide them in her large purse.

If she was feeling up to it, we might then make an expedition down to Grant Avenue—which could prove complicated because of the hoards of tourists. My grandmother, however, didn't mind them. In fact, it was as if they had spent all their money and traveled all the way across America simply to entertain her. It would have been better at those times if she could have spoken in Chinese; but for my sake, she would use English. Much to my acute embarrassment, she would point at a passing tourist only a yard away and announce in a loud voice to me, "Look at that funny red hair. Is it real?"

She treated the expensive art stores with the same enthusiasm. She would walk into a store that sold expensive jade or ivory carvings and act as if it were a museum, ignoring the frowns from owners and clerks until we had made a complete circuit of their establishment. Eventually, though, we would reach her real goal and make her purchases—sometimes it was the store that sold Chinese sausage, *lop cheong*. Then we would retrace the route back to her apartment, observing more tourists on the way.

Occasionally we might also stop at her social club, where she would show off her family to the other club members. At the club, though, she liked to light an incense stick at the altar and say a silent prayer—something that I, a Catholic in those days, felt uncomfortable about.

As a result, I did my best to show that I was different, becoming one of those obnoxious children who had to have a fork instead of chopsticks at a banquet in Chinatown—I didn't learn how to use chopsticks until I was twelve. I also insisted on having Coca-Cola instead of tea.

There are so many things that I did as a child that I regret now. My father gave me the wooden box with the cunning lock that he used when he came to America. On the bottom were the original customs stickers; but I managed to scrape most of them off.

Before my parents bought the store, they had lived near Chinatown, as did most Chinese Americans. As a result, my brother had gone to St. Mary's Grammar School. Technically, the school was a Catholic mission to convert Chinese Americans into Catholics. Uncle Francis's children had also gone there so when it came to start kindergarten, my parents decided to enroll me there.

It wasn't always easy adjusting to Chinatown. Around the fourth grade, the nuns decided to imitate another school that their order ran. During the daytime, that other school offered an hour of French instruction. Now in the late afternoon, after regular classes, our school building went from a Catholic school to a Chinese one. Chinese teachers moved into the classrooms and taught there. However, the nuns decided to institute an hour of Chinese during the regular school day.

The result was a disaster for me. I was placed in the dummies' class where simple Chinese words were taught with even simpler ones. However, we spoke no Chinese at home so I didn't even know the teacher's basic commands. As a result, I had to watch the other students and take out a book when they did or put it away.

The simplest thing, of course, would have been to learn those basic words. However, having been an A- student in the American part of the curriculum, I resented being put into the dummies' class and forced to learn a foreign language.

Moreover, I hated the teacher who seemed to be this shrill witch who liked to beat children. To this day, I can't think of calligraphy lessons without wincing. In calligraphy, which is the art of Chinese writing, we would practice the strokes of a character, trying to make it look as pretty as possible. For those lessons, we bought special books of rice paper. Special inserts were placed behind them and then we got out our ink.

Now Chinese ink is as rich and black as poster paint. Scholars and true calligraphers have ink sticks which they mix themselves with water. They have a little ink stand with a well into which they put water and then rub the stick on the side until they have the ink blended the way they want. Most of the ink sticks also have a slight perfume smell.

However, schoolchildren simply buy their ink premixed in a bottle. You then bought a little container called a *mok-op* which was about the size of a woman's compact and came in various shapes and sizes. Some might be as simple as a plastic jar with a screw-on lid. Others might be made out of metal with a design on the top, some of them square, others circular. Inside was a wad of cotton that was soaked in ink that was so thick that you could keep adding water without diluting it noticeably. Into this you would dip your brush and trace the strokes of the characters.

One classmate extravagantly used a bottle of ink. Unfortunately, as the teacher passed by one day, my classmate or my teacher knocked it over, ruining the Chinese silk dress the teacher was wearing.

She lectured us angrily in broken English. I gather that she had little use for American-born Chinese who were all lazy and disrespectful. And I suppose by the standards back in China we probably were.

Resenting both the teacher and the situation, I went out of my way to pass the course but not learn Chinese. Each week, we had a new lesson in the reader that we were expected to memorize, recite aloud, and then write out. So each week, I memorized a new pattern of sounds like a song and a new pattern of pictures like a cartoon. I wound up doing more work than anyone else in that class but I achieved my purpose: I passed without learning Chinese. The irony, of course, is that even if I had learned Chinese in that class, I wouldn't necessarily have been able to hold a conversation with my grandmother. She spoke the *Say-yup*, or four districts, dialect—actually a subdialect from the Yan-ping district—while we were learning the *Sam-yup*, or three districts, dialect from Canton.

(Years later I tried to take a conversational Cantonese course, and found myself taking out my resentments on that teacher. I wasn't eight and wasn't about to be pushed around. When I felt my teacher was calling on me too much, I told him to call on someone else. And when we discussed various aspects of Chinese history we would get into arguments, so eventually I quit.)

I also tried to put my Chinese schoolteacher into a book, *Child of the Owl*. I had intended to show how mean she was; but writing is always a kind of balance. If the character is to be more than a cardboard cartoon, you have to see things from her or his own viewpoint. As I wrote her scenes, I began to see why she would think of me as being undisciplined and disrespectful.

So there I was with all of these strange, new pieces that my grandmother had presented to me: pieces that had to be put into the puzzle that was myself but no clue where those pieces were to go.

In part, to come up with some answers, I began to keep a file of family history. Whenever my mother, my uncle, my aunts, or my grandmother told family stories, I would try to remember them so I could write them down later. It was only years later when I began to piece things together that I began to understand just how difficult a journey it had been for my grandmother from China, through Ohio and West Virginia and finally to her little home in Chinatown.

More than anyone, I respected my grandmother. She had not only survived, but she had become her own person—which was something I wanted to do. Though I might not have been able to put my feelings into words, I suspected that it was not easy.

Trying to imagine my grandmother as a teenager and a new bride, I later created a character called Cassia Young, a rebel in China during the nineteenth century and an ancestress of Casey Young of *Child of the Owl*.

In two books, *Serpent's Children* and *Mountain Light*, I tried to write about her long, painful growth into a unique person. As Uncle Quail says in my novel, *Sea Glass*, "the knife that shapes us must also be the knife that cuts."

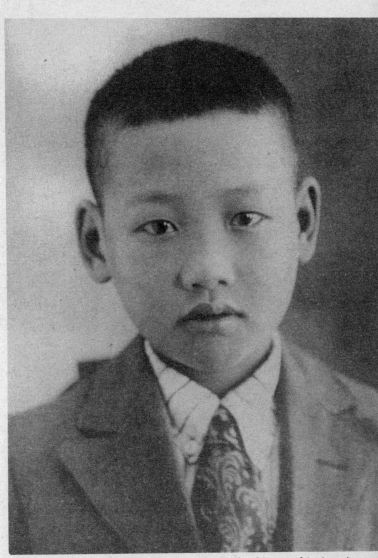
1923. My father, Thomas Yep, age 10, shortly after his arrival in America.

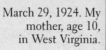

March 29, 1924. My
mother, age 10,
in West Virginia.

1949. My brother,
Spike, age 11,
and me.

1950. My father and I
on a picnic in
San Mateo.

1953. My father and I in front of Jezebel. Note the running
board behind us. I am wearing my version of a Robin Hood
outfit, complete with green shirt and green felt hat.

On the roof of
arl Apartments.
vearing my football
, complete with
ler pads and an
shioned toy leather
t.

My third grade photo.

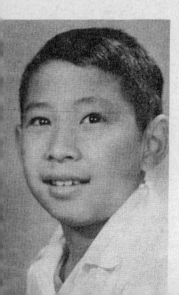

1959. My mother outside
the store. This was still the
period when she wore smocks.

1959. My father outside the store. These were among the first photos I took with our Ansco box camera. Note that the store is still La Conquista. Flies used to get trapped between the window and the cardboard advertisements.

1966. My senior year in high school. Outside the range of the camera, I am holding shut a one-size-fits-all tux.

The Pearl Apartments and our store. The signmaker has mistakenly spelled the name as "La Conquesta." Two of my nieces, Franny and Lisa, are standing by the doorway. Their mother, Terry, is leaning against the Mustang while my father is farther down the street, trying to stay out of the photo.

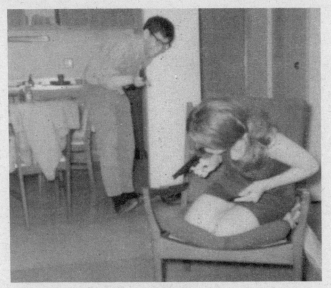
1968. Joanne and I in a water pistol fight.

Me in Sunnyvale in 1977.

Mother's Day, 1971. My grandmother, Marie Lee.

5

RAMBLING THROUGH AMERICA

THE REST of my relatives didn't seem to be as perplexed by the contradictions in being a Chinese American as I was. My own family had grown up as much American as Chinese. There had been a small number of families that had become established by the turn of the century so that my parents belonged to a generation that lived lives more or less like their white contemporaries. They played football, basketball, tennis, and all the other sports, and, in one family's big flat, they learned how to dance the newest dance crazes like the black bottom and the big apple. My mother and my aunts sang songs from Victor Herbert operettas at the Chinatown YWCA. In short, they did everything that white teenagers might do except they did it in Chinatown.

Although prejudice was more out in the open in those days,

my parents didn't feel forced to stay in Chinatown. When they were first married, they thought nothing of getting in a car and driving outside of Chinatown, going twenty miles away to San Mateo for milk shakes or going for picnics by the beach where they would roast potatoes.

So on the surface they were Americans who happened to be living in Chinatown. And yet there was something that remained Chinese and that went beyond speech patterns and food preferences. My parents always put studies before anything else and always showed deep respect for any of my teachers.

And there were also patterns that may be more personal than being Chinese and yet they are related. Whenever my father went into a restaurant, there was always an initial moment of anxiety—as if once he had physically crossed the threshold, he now had to cross a mental one. Years ago, when he and some friends had been outside of San Francisco, they had gone into a diner. The waitresses made a point of ignoring them no matter what they did because the service was only for whites. When my father and his friends finally left, the laughter pursued them.

The most Chinese of the family was my maternal grandfather, Sing Thin Lee, who could not speak any English. I remember him as a man with a broad smile who liked to watch me play but could never communicate with me. He asserted his authority only at Chinese New Year's when he would demand a freshly killed chicken. It was a duty that my mother and my aunts rotated among themselves because one of them would have to make sure it was freshly killed by being there when the neck was wrung.

He also insisted that we stop playing with guns at that time and avoid any other form of make-believe violence—I suppose for fear we might have violence during the coming year. As a family, we got together for every child's birthday, Christmas, Easter, and various other holidays; and at each we brought our guns and played cowboys or war. As a result of the artificial truce on our imaginations, Chinese New Year's could have been pretty boring. We couldn't expect a good dessert because chocolate cake wasn't part of the traditional Chinese menu. (That was one of the specialties of my mother's older sister, Mary Kim, who made everything from scratch. There were no store-bought mixes for her; and I have never had the equal of her cakes.)

Chinese New Year's was saved only by two things. One of them was greed because we could get a *li-see* which was a red envelope with some money inside, usually coins, but occasionally even dollar bills. Married people are supposed to give it out when you wish them wealth and prosperity with a hearty "*Gung hay fat choy.*"

The other thing was explosives. Until they were made illegal, firecrackers made up for the loss of any toy gun. They came in flat packets, wrapped in red or rose tissue paper with a colorful label glued to the top; and they ranged from the little lady fingers to the much larger sizes.

Lighting a string for a fuse, my cousins and I could set off the firecrackers individually one by one to draw out the exquisite pleasure; or we could set them off in strings in a single, sharp display. One time, my brother and older cousins even got hold of some dead old bush and strung firecrackers in it. They then rolled it down the hill, a bright ball of little lights occasionally leaping into the air with an explosion. It was most satisfying.

Nobody ever got hurt. We set off firecrackers under the watchful eyes of the adults. In fact, the uncles sometimes couldn't resist giving advice and even taking a lit string to help demonstrate what they meant. No one was stupid enough to light a firecracker in his or her hand; and certainly no one was dumb enough to throw a firecracker at one another.

And the next day, the steps outside my cousin's apartment

house would be ankle deep in red paper that would rustle as I shuffled through it, and lingering in the air would be the sad, nostalgic smell of gunpowder and singed paper.

My grandmother and my grandfather might have practiced the religious aspects of Chinese New Year's in private; but they had long-since given up with their American-born grandchildren—which probably made us wild Christian "heathens" in their eyes. For most of us, Chinese New Year's was eating and explosives.

For the older boys like my brother and some of my cousins, it also meant dancing in the dragon that has always been a fixture of the parade. There was a lump sum of money and a new pair of sneakers for running inside the dragon and helping it snake along Grant Avenue. The dragon dancers worked in teams, one team spelling the other during the ordeal. In the head would be someone with strong lungs who would smoke a cigar and exhale smoke from the dragon's mouth as he ran.

However, in some ways, I think the most typical Chinese American married my mother's sister, Rachel. Like my father, Uncle Francis had been born in China but managed to come over with his family somehow. My father said that he ran with a group of boys who were also foreign-born and they would have fights with the American-born Chinese—though as my father was quick to emphasize, it was only with fists and not with weapons. When Uncle Francis was young, his father had died so that, as the eldest son, Uncle Francis had been expected to take over as the head of the family.

As a teenager, he drove a laundry truck that he used in off-hours to transport his friends even though the truck could not be opened from inside in the back. Had there been an accident, the people inside the truck would have been trapped. (He was fond of saying later that he would never allow his kids to do what he had done.)

He became a car mechanic to support his growing family,

working for years on Studebakers. Later, when that company shut down, he tried to learn how to repair Volkswagen Beetles but found them too small and pinched, and switched over to trucks. Through sacrifice and hard work, he and Auntie Rachel managed to buy an apartment house in North Beach. Though their white neighbors were standoffish at first, most of them soon came around when they found out he was a car mechanic and was willing to work with them on their cars for free—a kind of desegregation with socket wrenches rather than court orders.

Years later, when I was working on a suspense book called, *Liar, Liar,* I called up Uncle Francis and timidly asked for some help. I needed to have a character die in a car crash and I wanted to get the facts straight. However, I wasn't sure if he would be insulted if I asked for advice in murdering someone.

To my surprise, Uncle Francis got quite enthusiastic about the process. Right away he told me to forget the movies where the villain slips under a car and cuts the line with the brake fluid. A good forensic scientist would look at the metal pipe and see the even edges of the break and know that someone had sabotaged the pipe. Uncle Francis, though, worked out a way to hide the sabotage, for which I was always grateful.

Of all of the family, Uncle Francis was the one with the itchiest of feet. The immigrant boy came to love his adopted country; and as a man, he couldn't see enough of America— especially its national parks with their canyons and their forests. He and his family chugged all over America in the old cars he kept running with his mechanical skills.

He took his greatest pleasure, though, in scenery that involved large bodies of water. He would drive for several hours all the way up to Clear Lake to catch a certain type of fresh fish that his mother liked. There, he would sit in his rowboat for hours, staring meditatively out at the blue water.

Other times, he would go to the ocean and fish for abalone,

which is a kind of sea fish that crawls along the rocks under water and eats the seaweed. Legally, he could only take abalone that were over a certain length—seven inches for the red abalone and five inches for the black. However, to reach that size, an abalone had to be fairly clever, staying at depths that humans wouldn't usually reach. As a result, Uncle Francis would have to go out at the extreme low tides no matter what time of night it was or how cold the ocean might be. It meant diving some eight feet or so into the dark, cold water and, with the little abalone bar that hung from his wrist, prying the abalone off the rock, taking care that the abalone did not clamp down over his fingers, perhaps trapping him.

Diving also had other hazards. There were certain bays where he wouldn't go for fear of sharks; and other areas would draw seals who would be curious about the hunt—but then Uncle Francis was also known to pull a leg.

Once he had the abalone, he had to rise to the surface and go to the beach where Auntie Rachel would have a fire going so that Uncle Francis could warm up. Though I never went diving with Uncle Francis, my brother did. He said that Uncle Francis, who was bald, would come out of the water blue from the top of his head to the bottom of his feet.

Before *Liar, Liar*, I had consulted Uncle Francis for another book, *Sea Glass*, because I wanted to write about a Chinese abalone fisherman, Uncle Quail. I had had my fill of the fake wisdom that was put by American writers in the mouths of supposed Chinese masters—such as the master on the television series, *Kung Fu*. The old-timers had learned a good many things; but their lessons, like their manner of teaching, were likely to be rough-hewn.

In *Sea Glass*, there was a boy, Craig Chin, who was very much like myself—a klutz at sports and an outsider in his school. However, Uncle Quail teaches him to swim and in so doing, teaches him certain lessons of dignity and self-respect.

Uncle Quail was much like the abalone he caught—rough and ugly-looking on the outside of the shell and a shimmering rainbow within.

My wandering uncle also seemed to have the strangest adventures when he went camping. Once, at Yosemite National Park in California, Uncle Francis woke to feel something warm and rasping, rubbing at his head. Fortunately, he took a peek out of his sleeping bag first and saw that it was a bear who had mistook his head for a salt lick.

Another time, he went camping and was plagued with raccoons. On the last day, as he was breaking camp, he heard something rummaging around in the tent. Thinking it was yet another pesky raccoon, he went to the tent and kicked his bare foot inside shouting, "Scoot."

However, it wasn't a raccoon but a skunk; and it did what any self-respecting skunk would do: anoint Uncle Francis—or more specifically his foot. Even through his shoe and stocking, the smell was so overpowering that everyone insisted he stick his foot outside of the car window on the ride home. It was particularly noticeable since Uncle Francis was the one driving the car. Unfortunately for him, there was a highway patrolman around the next corner.

Uncle Francis got some of his most unusual traffic tickets that day. Even so, that didn't discourage him or prevent him from driving through America, encountering skunks, bears, and snakes wherever he went.

6

CHINATOWN

IF UNCLE FRANCIS and other members of our family left Chinatown to explore America, my experience was the reverse because I was always going into Chinatown to explore the streets and perhaps find the key to the pieces of the puzzle. But the search only seemed to increase the number of pieces.

When I was a boy, Chinatown was much more like a small town than it is now. It was small not only in terms of population but in physical area as well. Its boundaries were pretty well set by Pacific Avenue on the north next to the Italian neighborhood of North Beach, Kearny Street on the east, Sacramento Street on the south, and Stockton Street on the west—an area only of a few city blocks.

There is a stereotype that the Chinese lived in Chinatown because they wanted to. The fact was that before the fair housing laws they often had no choice.

For years there was a little cottage on an ivy-covered hill in the southwest corner of Chinatown just above the Stockton tunnel. There was—and still is—very little plant life in Chinatown so the only color green I saw was the paint on my school. The kind of green that is alive—lawns, bushes, and trees—was something I had to leave Chinatown to see, except for that ivy-covered slope. On windy days, the ivy itself would stir and move like a living sea; and overlooking the ivy was a cottage that was charm itself. However, as much as I admired the house—on occasion I was disloyal enough to the Pearl Apartments to want to live in it—I knew it wasn't for us. My Auntie Mary had once tried to rent it and had been refused because she was Chinese.

Out of some forty-five or so students in my class, I was one of the few who lived outside of Chinatown. Now, thanks to the fair housing laws that were passed in the 1960s, almost none of my former classmates live there; and Chinatown itself has spilled out of its traditional boundaries.

When I was a boy, though, we could see the results of white money and power on three sides of us. To the east we could stare up at the high-rise office buildings of the business district; and to the west, up the steep streets, were the fancy hotels of Nob Hill. Southward lay downtown and the fancy department stores.

Grant Avenue led directly to downtown; but for years I always thought of the Stockton tunnel as the symbolic end to Chinatown. When it had been cut right through a hill, my father and his young friends had held foot races through it after midnight, hooting and hollering so that the echoes seemed to be the cheers of a huge crowd. The rich white world began just on the other side of the tunnel.

There were also invisible barriers that separated the wealthy whites from the Chinese who cleaned their apartments or waited on their tables. The Chinese could see and even touch the good life; but they could not join in.

One of my classmates, Harold, had a paper route on Nob Hill. I still find it hard to believe that, up hills that angled some forty degrees or so, he carried a kind of poncho loaded with papers in front and back. But he did that every afternoon. Once I went along with him; and I followed him into one of the fanciest hotels on Nob Hill, past the elaborately uniformed doorman, over the plush carpets, under the ornate chandeliers, and around in back, down concrete hallways as bleak as the ones in the Chinatown housing projects that were painted a cheap, gaudy yellow—a shade which my friend referred to as "landlord yellow." Harold would deliver the afternoon newspapers to the laundrymen and other workers. And with my friend that day, I wandered all around the roots of that palatial dream of wealth.

When the poncho was flat, my friend and I returned to his tenement apartment where there was only one toilet to a floor; and the toilet lacked both a door and toilet paper. When you went, you brought in your own toilet paper. Nothing could be done about the door except changing your attitude about privacy.

Many of my schoolmates lived in the Chinatown projects; and I wasn't sure if life was any better in them than life in the projects near our store. Another newspaper carrier named Paul lived there. As the oldest boy, Paul was expected to look after his younger brothers and sisters while his parents worked—a common practice among many Chinese families. However, as a result, Paul had failed to develop many social skills let alone improve his English. I remember the nun sending him out on an errand and then asking the rest of the class to act as his special friend—which was easy for her to say because she was an adult.

As far as I knew, he hung around with his own group in the projects rather than with anyone from school. His group, though, must have been pretty rough because one of them threw a knife that "accidentally" hit Paul in the eye. Fortunately, there was a charity that arranged an operation; and he was given a new eye from someone who had recently died.

We never knew the identity of the donor; but Paul amused himself by claiming it was a rich white. First, he would clap a hand over his new eye and roll his remaining Chinese eye around. Then he would put his hand over his old one and gaze around elaborately with his new American eye. And then he would announce to us that the world looked just the same whether it was a Chinese eye or an American one.

Paul had shot up early and was a giant compared to the rest of us. When he ran, he looked like an ostrich with arms. He would kick out his legs explosively while his arms flailed the air, so it was hard not to laugh; but we didn't because he was also immensely strong.

The playground at St. Mary's was only a concrete basketball court below. Up above, there was a kind of patio between the convent and the school where the younger children could play. However, the nuns were so worried about our knocking one another down that they forbade us to run during recess. About the only thing we could play under those conditions was a kind of slow-motion tag.

At noon, we could go across the street to the Chinese Playground—the playground where my father had once been the director. In those days, it consisted of levels. The first level near the alley that became known as Hang Ah Alley was a volleyball and a tennis court. Down the steps was the next level with a sandbox (which was usually full of fleas), a small director's building, a Ping-Pong table, an area covered by tan bark that housed a slide, a set of bars, and a set of swings and other simple equipment. The level next to the Chinese Baptist church was the basketball court.*

*Years later, as part of a set of improvements, the city built an elaborate jungle gym in the playground which upset a number of the older Chinese. "What do they think our children are? Monkeys?"

We had Physical Education once a week there. The playground director taught the boys, and I suppose the nun handled the girls. Sometimes it was calisthenics, other times it was baseball played with a tennis ball on the tennis court. There was no pitcher. Rather, the "batter" threw up the ball and hit it with his fist. Because of his size and added arm strength from his own paper route, Paul could hit a home run almost every time, sending the tennis ball flying over the high wire mesh fence.

However, my experience was frequently the reverse. Because the present director knew that my father had once been the director of the playground, he was always urging me on to one disaster after another.

The worst happened when he wasn't present though. In third grade, we had a very sweet nun, Sister Bridget, who used to play kickball with us. Kickball was like baseball except that the pitcher bowled a ball the size of a basketball over the ground and the "batter" kicked it. One time someone kicked a ball so that it rolled foul. Retrieving it, I threw it to sister; but as fate would have it, she had turned her head right at that moment to look at something else. I wound up hitting her in the head; and though there was no physical harm, I broke her glasses. Even though my parents paid for replacements, the rest of my class treated me as if I were taboo for striking a nun. I learned what it meant to be shunned and to be invisible.

The experience also reinforced my belief that I was terrible at sports. Despite all the practice and coaching from my father, I was hopeless when it came to catching any ball in any shape or size. Nor could I dribble a basketball, even though my father sometimes kept me practicing in the little courtyard until it was almost too dark to see.

The only sport that I was remotely good at was football. Having worked and lifted crates in the store made me fairly strong. As a result, I was a good lineman at blocking and rushing—like my hero, Leo Nomellini. However, I was still hopeless at catching a pass. I still remember one game where I dropped three touchdown passes in a row. I was so bad that our opponents stopped covering me. Our quarterback, unable to resist a wide-open target, persisted in throwing to me—and I dropped yet a fourth pass that could have been a touchdown.

The fact that my whole family was athletic only added to my disgrace. My father had played both basketball and football. My mother had also played basketball as well as being a track star, winning gold medals at the Chinese Olympics—a track event held for Chinese Americans. My brother was also excellent at basketball as well as bowling. Even worse, my father had coached championship teams when he had been a director at Chinese Playground—the very site of most of my failures. I often felt as if I were a major disappointment to my family.

Moreover, my lack of Chinese made me an outsider in Chinatown—sometimes even among my friends. Since it was a Catholic school taught by nuns, my friends would always tell dirty jokes in Chinese so the nuns wouldn't understand. However, neither did I, so I missed out on a good deal of humor when I was a boy. What Chinese I did pick up was the Chinese that got spoken in the playground—mostly insults and vulgar names.

There were times even with a good friend like Harold when I felt different. Though Harold and I would go see American war movies, he could also open up a closet and show me the exotic Chinese weapons his father, a gardener, would fashion in his spare time and I could sense a gulf between my experience and that of Harold's. It was as if we belonged to two different worlds.

Even my friends' games and entertainments in Chinatown could sometimes take their own different spin. They weren't quite like the games I saw American boys playing on television or read about in Homer Price. Handball was played with the all-purpose tennis ball against a brick wall in the courtyard.

Nor do I remember anyone ever drawing a circle with chalk and shooting marbles in the American way. Instead, someone would set up marbles on one side of the basketball court at St. Mary's and invite the others to try to hit them. If they did, they got the marbles. If they didn't the boy would quickly snatch up their shooters. The ideal spot, of course, was where irregularities in the paving created bumps or dips to protect the owner's marbles. At times, one edge of the courtyard would resemble a bazaar with different boys trying to entice shooters to try their particular setup with various shouted jingles.

Other times, they would set up baseball or football cards. Trading cards weren't meant to be collector's items; but were used like marbles. In the case of cards, the shooter would send a card flying with a flick of the wrist. Mint cards did not always fly the truest; and certain cards with the right bends and folds became deadly treasures.

But that sense of being different became sharpest the time I was asked to sing. Our school had a quartet that they sent around to build goodwill. The two girls and two boys dressed up in outfits that were meant to be Chinese: the girls in colored silk pajamas and headdresses with pom-poms, the boys in robes with black vests and caps topped by red knobs.

However, one day in December, one of the boys took sick so the nuns chose me to take his place. Musical ability was not a consideration; the fit of the costume was the important thing. We were brought to sing before a group of elderly people. I can remember following a cowboy with an accordion and a cowgirl with a short, spangled skirt who sang Christmas carols with a country twang.

Then we were ushered out on the small stage and I could look out at the sea of elderly faces. I think they were quite charmed with the costumed Chinese children. Opening their mouths, the others began to sing in Chinese. Now during all this, no one had bothered to find out if I could sing, let alone sing in Chinese. I recognized the tune as "Silent Night" but the words were all in Chinese. I tried to fake it but I was always one note and one pretend-syllable behind the others. Then they swung into "It Came Upon a Midnight Clear." This time they sang in English so I tried to sing along and ranged all over the musical scale except the notes I was supposed to be singing. Finally, one of the girls elbowed me in the ribs and from the side of her mouth, she whispered fiercely, "Just mouth the words."

Up until then I had enjoyed putting on costumes and even had a variety of hats, including cowboy and Robin Hood outfits as well as a French Foreign Legion hat and a Roman helmet; but the experience cured me of wanting to dress up and be something else. How could I pretend to be somebody else when I didn't even know who I was?

In trying to find solutions, I had created more pieces to the puzzle: the athlete's son who was not an athlete, the boy who got "A's" in Chinese school without learning Chinese, the boy who could sing neither in key nor in Chinese with everyone else.

7

THE
OUTSIDER

YEARS AGO, my brother had once bought a Chinese puzzle as a gift for a friend. It was one of those boxes with interlocking pieces of wood. Using the instructions, my brother separated the pieces and opened up the box and then put the instructions in the center, carefully locking all the pieces back together again before he wrapped it up for his friend.

The more time I spent going back and forth between my own neighborhood, the more I felt as if I was like that box with the necessary instructions locked up inside me and no way to get at them.

One of the reasons I became a Catholic was to obtain some guidance. Out of our large class, I don't think we ever had more than a dozen Catholics; and of that group of Catholics, I don't think one of us had been baptized as an infant. However,

I not only became a Catholic but an altar boy as well.

Like many other altar boys in those days, I dutifully memorized the Latin without learning the meaning of the words and went without further study into the bewildering maze of Catholic ritual. Since there were such few altar boys and so many ceremonies, we were stretched rather thin and there was a good deal that had not been covered in basic training.

At our meetings, Father would work out schedules and hand out assignments with the most fanciful titles such as the "boat" (the one who carried the vessel that held the raw incense) and the "thurible" (the one with the bowl-like vessel in which the incense actually burned). The thurible was fun in a way, because it was a globe, the upper half of which slid up on a set of chains. The real trick was lighting the little charcoal briquette quickly. Since we often had to double up on duties, we were frequently pressed for time. As a result, we would solemnly walk with folded hands until we reached the door of the sacristy—where we dressed and the various accessories were kept. However, as soon as we were through the doorway, it was a mad dash to light the charcoal so we could get back outside in time for our next cue. Generally we held the charcoal over a match holding the edge near the flame until we saw little red lines where the charcoal had caught fire. Dropping it quickly into the thurible and slamming the top down, we then swung it wildly in a circle so that more of the charcoal would catch. The true miracle each week was probably that we didn't burn down the chapel.

Father put up with a good deal from me as an altar boy. I think in my first or second week, I was expected to be the master of ceremonies, which meant I had to help Father dress in special vestments outside on the altar before a certain ceremony. No one had warned me; and I had never paid enough attention when I had seen the ceremony before. Since Father put on most of his vestments by sliding them over his head, I assumed this vestment was the same way. However, in reality it was more like a shawl that I should have simply draped around his shoulders. As a result, I tried to jam it over his head while I hunted desperately for the hole in the garment until in exasperation he grabbed it from me and put it on himself. Unfortunately, Father McGuire was bald and so all of my maneuvers had buffed and rubbed his head to a high sheen.

Even when I was more experienced, Father could never be quite sure of what would happen. Once the ladies of the altar society took out all the small- and medium-sized cassocks and sent them to the cleaners. We were all too short, though, for the remaining large cassocks so Father supplied some pins. None of us had much experience at pinning up anything, so about halfway through Mass, the pins began to drop out of the black, dresslike cassocks. Every time we knelt, stood up, or genuflected, we could hear a ping as a pin popped to the rug. Halfway through Mass, we were stumbling around the altar like so many clowns, unable to find our footing in the yards of black cloth that engulfed our feet.

Nor was Father particularly upset when I set fire to the altar itself. We had a kind of pole with a bell at one end to extinguish the candles. Branching from the other side was a long waxed wick that could be extended with a knob. After it had been lit, I was supposed to use it to light the candles on the altar. However, I utilized too long a section of wick so that the whole section suddenly caught on fire and dropped on top of the altar. I think it was Father who put out the fire as I stood there in horror at what I had done. Fortunately, it only burned through the white altar cloth, which the ladies of the parish later repaired.

Again, early on in my serving days, I was part of a ceremony in which we were supposed to strip the altar bare. The Mass and ceremony were long ones and very solemn; but I had acquitted myself well until it was time to take out the drop cloths at the front of the altar. Our chapel altar was like a long table. A drop cloth hung at the front from a frame; and the drop cloths were of different colors to match the vestments that Father was supposed to wear that day. Father unhooked the first drop cloth and rolled up the cloth on the long pole and handed it to me.

Unfortunately, the pole was twice my height and so it was difficult to balance. Instead of walking solemnly to the sacristy where the cloths were to be stowed, I lurched, almost taking out some of the other servers who managed to get out of the way just in time. Like a drunken lancer, I struck one side of the doorway. Thrown off balance, I staggered back as everyone ducked. Even more determined, I took aim and tried to charge through the sacristy door but missed and hit the other side of the doorway. By the time I actually made it through the door, even the nuns were laughing.

Ultimately, it was the Chinatown branch library rather than the Catholic Church that held out the possibility of a solution—if only in my imagination. Both my parents were good readers, going through the four dailies—the *Chronicle*, the *Examiner*, the *News*, and the *Call-Bulletin*. Moreover, they had raised me to think of reading as a pleasure. They would either read one of our children's books or a comic book to me; and the rule was that I had to read a story back to them for each one they read to me. One of my first three-syllable words was "obnoxious," which I picked up from a *Little Lulu* story.* The best way to punish me was not to read to me. Now that I had my own library card, I had even more material to read.

The Chinatown library was especially handy because I could

---

*I once met a librarian who had read the same story and called her brother "obnoxious," which drove him crazy because their parents would not tell him what the word meant and he was too stubborn to look it up in a dictionary.

clamber onto the cable car with my haul of checked-out books and begin my ride home.

The library was then and still is a picturesque stone building with cable cars rattling just outside. The layout has changed over the years; but in those days, the children's books were housed in a room behind the main desk.

I particularly remember two librarians who were usually at the desk, one of them was a Chinese woman whose makeup peeled off in little flakes to reveal tan skin underneath. She never seemed to smile—as if afraid of cracking her makeup any further. I used to hold my breath when she would check out my books, waiting to see if any more of her makeup would split and fall off like an iceberg from a glacier.

The other was a local celebrity, the Answer Man. One of the local radio stations used to call him with questions the audience had sent in and he would answer them from the resources in the library. Checking out a book from him was always an ordeal because he would quiz me about the words in the title. I usually knew the answers but was too tongue-tied to speak to such a famous person.

I'm ashamed to say that I don't remember the children's librarian. I remember having someone try to interest me in *Homer Price and His Doughnut Machine*. However, I could never get interested in it or books like that. My reality consisted of apartments and houses crowding right up to the sidewalk—so American suburbs with their ranch houses and lawns and trees seemed as exotic as Hawaii to me.

It was also strange to me that Homer Price and all his friends had bicycles. In my experience, a bicycle was something you rented to ride in the park; and quite a few children used to learn how to ride bicycles in the big parking lot outside Kezar Stadium. Across the street were a number of bicycle shops that would rent out bicycles for the day so you could explore Golden Gate Park, which was just beyond Kezar Stadium.

Quite a few of my friends had learned how to ride bicycles in that manner. My father had valiantly attempted to teach me one Sunday afternoon; but I had come out of the humiliating experience with bruises that covered my backside and with legs scraped raw.

In any event, the muni buses, electric streetcars, cable cars, and trolleys were far more efficient for getting around in hilly San Francisco. Again, since most of my friends lived in the projects or small apartments, bicycles were difficult to store and difficult to keep from being stolen. In fact, I only knew two people who had bicycles. One was a classmate, Jimmy, who used it to escape Chinatown, pedaling as far south as San Mateo. The other was my brother who had been a Western Union messenger.**

Even so, as I said earlier, I also wanted to consider myself an American. It would be logical to assume that I would treat the Homer Price books as my manuals on how to be an American boy.

However, there was one thing in the Homer Price books that I found too preposterous to swallow—and this despite a strong tolerance for the incredible. (Going back and forth between Chinatown and my neighborhood had taught me not to make too many assumptions about anything. In fact, I could suspend disbelief enough to enjoy the Freddy the Pig series. Farms already seemed like fantasy places to me so that it wasn't too hard to imagine that animals could talk there.)

Even so, I couldn't abide one thing in Homer Price or books like them: all the children left their front doors unlocked. No one I knew *did* that—either in my neighborhood or in China-

---

**The telephone has made them superfluous; but, at one time, if people wanted to send a message to a friend in a faraway city, they would send a telegram to a Western Union office in that place. Then a messenger would personally deliver the telegram to that friend.

town. It was one thing to be fantastical; it was quite another to be dumb. Leaving doors unlocked went counter to my knowledge of human nature. More, it offended my rules for survival so that I found the Homer Price books too ridiculous to enjoy.

Reading, though, was always intimately bound up with asthma. I have had asthma since I can remember. I once almost walked out on a famous movie because the actor in the scene was simply panting and yet the movie called it an asthma attack. A real asthma attack is like suffocating in an invisible coffin. The air is out there but you cannot draw it in through the unseen walls no matter how hard your chest heaves and your lungs work.

When I had one of my attacks, my parents would call Dr. Bepler. She was a fine, old-fashioned family doctor who still made house calls. (In fact, she wound up taking care of three generations of my family, my oldest niece being one of the last children Dr. Bepler delivered before she retired.) During a bad asthma attack, she would come in with her black bag and her big, reassuring smile and tell me she was going to chase away the "Wheezles" as she called one of my attacks. Then she would give me a shot that would ease my breathing and give me ten pennies for being so brave about the shot.

However, she often could not come right away and before she could arrive and sometimes after a visit, there were long nights when I could not sleep even if I was sitting propped up in bed. My father would pick up a newspaper and anxiously fan me, trying to get more wind into my lungs; and more importantly my mother would read to me.

Among the books we owned was *The Pirates of Oz*, which was a continuation of Baum's original stories by Ruth Plumy Thompson. It was a long book compared to the others so my parents hadn't read it to me before. However, during a prolonged attack, my mother began to read the chapters to fill the long hours. Exhausted from a lack of sleep, I drifted into a kind of half-sleep where I could not always separate the story from my own dreams. At one point, the asthma was so severe that I was convinced I was going to die; but as I slipped into a half-sleep, I fell into a strange logic of dreams and reasoned that I could not die because my story had not yet come to an end.

As a result, I quickly discovered the other Oz books in the Chinatown branch and devoured them eagerly. They were housed on two lower shelves of the children's room near the doorway. The brown linoleum near the shelves was worn thin. When I couldn't find all of the series there, I starting haunting the Main Library down near City Hall because the collection there was complete.

It was an imposing building when I was a child, covering nearly all of a city block, with a grand marble staircase that led up to the second floor. The children's room was down a hallway to the right of the staircase. I already knew the way because my mother used to take me there on our afternoon excursions though it was sometimes hard to park while they were building an underground garage and convention center. People referred to it as Mole Hall because of the huge mounts of dirt that towered above the street.

Though I really couldn't have put my feelings into words at the time, I think I loved the Oz books because they seemed far more real to me than the Homer Price books. The Oz books gave me a way to think about myself.

In the Oz books, you usually have some child taken out of his or her everyday world and taken to a new land where he or she must learn new customs and adjust to new people. There was no time for being stunned or for complaining. The children took in the situation and adapted. Unlike the Homer Price books, the Oz books talked about survival. They dealt with the real mysteries of life—like finding yourself and your place in the world. And that was something I tried to do every day I got on and off the bus.

From fantasy, it was natural to begin reading science fiction. At that time, every science-fiction book was marked by a rocket ship on the spine; and I would go through the children's room at the Chinatown and North Beach branches as well as the Main Library, looking for anything with a blue rocket on its spine. I moved quickly on to the young adult science-fiction books. Robert Heinlein was an author I liked because his characters were so funny and memorable.

However, Andre Norton was a special favorite because she could evoke whole new worlds with a kind of sadness and wonder. Up until then, I had not really thought that much about stars because I saw only a few in the night sky. San Francisco's lights were too bright and hid most of them. On some of our expeditions, my mother had taken me to Morrison Planetarium in the park to see stars; but I did not see the real thing until my first trip to Disneyland. We took the train, called the Lark, to Los Angeles and slept in a Pullman car. Kept awake by the clackety-clack of the train wheels, I leaned over from my berth and peeked out under the shade. For the first time in my life, I saw a blaze of stars spilled out over the black sky. I didn't sleep much that night between the noise, the excitement of seeing Disneyland, and the display of stars.

Unfortunately, stars were something that people had to drive to see. I only saw them when I went on camping trips, either with my parents to Yosemite or with the Boys' Club.

Anyway, the real appeal of Norton's books was not the stars themselves but the exotic worlds she created with their mysterious, half-ruined cities. I already knew what it was like to see an area that had been abandoned. Half the fun of her books wasn't so much the plot or the characters but the universe itself she created. And through that sad, tragic landscape ran outlaws and outcasts with whom I could identify.

My imagination, though, was often exercised in other ways. Because my brother was so much older than I was and my parents would sometimes be working down in the store, I was often by myself. I had inherited my brother's army of bottle caps. Soda was sold in various bottles and there was a bottle opener attached to the shelves near the refrigerator with a box below that. From that box, I drafted the recruits for my armies with the more common caps becoming the foot soldiers and the rarer caps serving as officers and generals.

Later, I began to acquire real toy soldiers when my mother would take me to a wonderful toy store called the World of Toys on Fillmore Street where they sold boxes of Britains lead soldiers. I still have many of them, much nicked, dented, and scraped over the years.

As with anything, the set up was half the fun, creating a battlefield out of an old quilt thrown on the floor, and forts and buildings built from Lincoln logs. In time, I went from individual battles to entire campaigns and even wars; and often the background became as important as the warfare.

However, one drawback of being alone with just my imagination was that I could often scare myself. Left alone, I could often imagine that the furniture and other objects were coming to life. Often from the corner of my eye, it seemed as if some chair or table had moved. The nightmares in *Poltergeist* were close to my own and I frequently planned where I was going to take refuge, working out elaborate escape routes that would take me to the top of cabinets or inside a closet.

A couple of times these scary fantasies took on a tinge of reality: once when I saw men's silhouettes on the fire escape, and another time when I looked through the windowpanes of our apartment door and saw strange men in the hallway. In both cases, they were burglars checking out the apartment house for future break-ins. In one case, my father thwarted them by putting up chicken wire between our building and the others so it was impossible to get up to our roof and down our fire escapes. In the other case, he broke the buzzer mechanism on the building's front door. In safer times, it had been possible to be up in your apartment and push a button that would unlock the front door downstairs for visitors.

By the time I was in the sixth grade, though, I had outgrown most of my imaginary fears, and had also gotten some company. My brother had gotten married to a girl from St. Mary's, Terry Lee. They had met at one of the dances there. Once they were married they often took me along when they went to see movies—whether it was their idea or not. Shortly after that, they had a daughter, Francine, named after my mother, Franche. Francine was ten years younger than me—just as I was ten years younger than my brother.

The first grandchild, Francine often had all of us dancing with her; and since she liked to sing "Happy Birthday," we put candles on anything so we could sing it, including apple pies. However, when I would have one of my battlefields set up, she could tear through it like Godzilla through Tokyo so my parents bought a portable gate which could be placed over the doorway. Poor Franny would stand mournfully outside the gate, holding onto the bars like some prisoner on death row. Once she leaned so hard that the entire gate fell over. Quickly she jumped to her feet, set the gate back into the doorway, and resumed leaning mournfully as before. She was more like a pesky little sister than a niece.

I was also able to turn my own imagination to good use. The Boys' Club was a club for teenagers with a clubhouse that had been set up underneath the chapel. The Junior Boys' Club was for preteens.

Like most groups in the mission, we were chronically short on money and would raise funds by putting on skits. Mercifully, none of the scripts have survived, only photos; but in one skit I dressed up as Alley Oop the caveman (the hero of a comic strip who had been immortalized in a rock-and-roll tune) while someone else lip-synced to the song.

The plays were awful, consisting of one pun strung after another without any logical plot. I remember writing a parody on a popular television crime show back then, *The Untouchables*, which I called *The Uneatables*. Ironically, it was included in a dinner show where we served up masses of spaghetti.

However, we not only had to write, produce, and act in the shows, we also had to sell the tickets because the point was to raise money. The best spot was in front of the church, Old St. Mary's. Having survived the earthquake and fire of 1906, it was a historical monument. It stood at the real beginning of Chinatown and had a cable car running right outside. Put all those elements together and you have a magnet that draws tourists like iron shavings.

By that time, I was an old veteran at selling—having had to hawk everything from Christmas seals to candy. There was a certain friendly, wide-eyed expression that I looked for on a tourist's face because it meant that he or she had just arrived in town, was feeling good, and was ready to part with money on a charitable impulse.

One time I saw a man with his wife and several daughters. They had the "look" so I walked up to them with a smile and went into my spiel. The father turned to his family and said, "It might be fun to see a Chinese show while we're in Frisco."

I should have warned him right away; but when I realized he was going to buy a book of tickets, I remained silent. However, over the next few days, I became increasingly uncomfortable over what I had done. The night of the show itself, I kept peeking out of one side of the curtain. Most of the audience were schoolmates or family so it was almost all Chinese. Then, to my acute embarrassment, the auditorium doors swung open and in came the tourist family. They had come expecting some fanciful display of Chinese culture and instead got a junkman's load of bad puns. I don't think those poor people lasted to intermission; but at least they had the kindness not to ask for a refund—though I occasionally wondered if that man's family ever trusted his judgment in entertainment again.

It was also around that time, having exhausted the children's and young adult books, that I went into the adult science-fiction section. Naturally excited, I would talk about the ideas and plots with my friends—no matter how wild or outrageous they might be. In the eighth grade, I became particularly good friends with one of my classmates. Though he had a lot of good qualities, he had one habit that was not always kind: He repeated whatever gossip he heard about me. From him I heard that our classmate, Tim, thought I was "weak-minded" for liking science fiction.***

In a way, I had asked for just such an opinion. In fact, one could even say it was true because I was not particularly practical; and yet it still hurt. I was so ashamed that I never tried to ask Tim if the gossip was true. Nor did I have any idea how many other of my close friends might share that opinion and did not dare ask.

However, what had once made me feel so comfortable now made me feel insecure. Then, too, as an eighth-grader, I was particularly sensitive to feeling like an alien myself. As a result, though I was afraid of leaving grammar school for high school, part of me was also glad of new beginnings.

***Years later I had my revenge because Tim's son liked my science fiction.

8

PUZZLE SOLVING

ST. IGNATIUS was a boy's high school founded in 1855, which made it old for San Francisco. It was a hulking three-story building of stones that sat on the Stanyan Street hill. Down the slope lay the Haight-Ashbury, where flower power was being born in places like the coffeehouse called "The Blue Unicorn." But behind our high school's stone walls we were sheltered from most of those changes.

I'd had white friends when I was small—before the projects had been built and their families moved away. However, St. Ignatius High School was the first time I had ever been with so many whites.

My cousin Gregory, who was a year ahead of me, had trouble his first year. Seating was alphabetical so he had wound up sitting most of the time in front of a boy who hated Asians and who had tried to make Gregory's life miserable.

However, I was fortunate enough to be protected from much of that because I was put into an honors class my freshman year. We were all ambitious to some degree so good grades were a means of earning respect. Grades were also so important that my parents let me out of hated chores in the store during the school year; and I was eager to do well so I would not have to go back to putting cans of beer in the icebox. As a result, I received good grades.

I was also fortunate that most of us freshmen were about the same size. Though I couldn't dribble a basketball and catch a pop fly to save my life, I could play intramural football as a lineman—the really big bruisers went out for the frosh-soph team. Moreover, years of my father's instruction had taught me that even if you couldn't do something well you could at least "hustle"—an attitude that also stood me in good stead. (I gave up playing football the next fall when I found out that most of the intramural football players had grown another three inches and were twenty pounds heavier.)

While there were boys there who never managed to climb out of the pit their own prejudices had dug for them—like the one my cousin had encountered—most were willing to correct their impressions once they got to know me. In the first few weeks, a classmate by the name of Steel asked me, "How come you can talk English so good?"

It was clear that Steel was not in the honors class for his skills in English; and I had enough sense not to correct his grammar. As it turned out, my family had already been in America for several generations before Steel's family had come from Poland—and promptly changed their names to Steel.

Racism wasn't so easy to avoid when it was in a teacher. The coach of one of our sports teams had once been put in charge of our study period during which he entertained us with stories of killing "gooks" in Korea. It was about halfway through the period before I realized that a gook was either a Korean or a Chinese; and I cringed the rest of the session.

Fortunately, it was the last study period he supervised. It was the early 1960s when the civil rights marches were going on and the younger Jesuits were especially sensitive to racial issues. When there was a bombing of a black church down South, they made sure there was a good turnout from the school at a memorial mass in a black neighborhood; and there were numerous other occasions when we were made aware of the larger issues.

My honors class, lacking the prestige that having a first-team varsity athlete gave a class, used to try to win the various school drives. Like all good Catholic schools, we had our chocolate wars; but we also had wars with everything else that could be used to raise money, including S & H Green stamps. (There was a period when stores gave out trading stamps when you purchased something. When you had enough stamps, you could use them to get various things from the stamp stores. In this case, though, it was musical instruments for the band.) It always seemed like every week there was some big roll of butcher paper in the school hallway with some kind of thermometer showing the progress of each class in that particular drive.

Each year we took a new nickname tied in to our class designation; and you were known by that name for the rest of the year either in intramural sports or drives or any other competition. Most other classes took names like 2C Cougars; but we also wound up with interesting names. In our junior year, we were the 3G Garbanzo Beans—the suggestion of a classmate who lobbied successfully for that name. At the time, none of us considered the fact that we would be identified throughout the year, on each drive chart and every intramural game, as "garbanzos."

My class was a group of funny, creative boys; and we had teachers to match. We learned American history from a Boston Irish who used to thunder at us rather than lecture—which was fine for stories about the Civil War but not for the intricacies of the Taft-Hartley Act.

Our history teacher had two pet peeves: President Franklin Delano Roosevelt and Coca-Cola. He suspected that President Roosevelt had died before his fourth term and that an actor had replaced him. Trying to prove he was wrong, I accepted his challenge and began to do library research that led to long, earnest discussions with Mr. Vincent the mortician concerning the preparation of corpses. While I was never able to prove or disprove my teacher's suspicions, it seemed at one time there had been a wide number of people who had shared his beliefs.

In any event, he was more concerned with the way that Coca-Cola was undermining the strength of America's youth and spoke against it at every opportunity in his deep growl. He told us of a B-24 bomber during World War II that had crash landed at the airfield. When the fire truck and ambulances had raced out to the wreck, they found that the plane had no bullet holes. Inside, the bomber crew was all dead without a mark on them, only empty bottles of Coca-Cola rolling around on the floor of the plane.

However, it was our science teachers who were especially memorable. I took physics from a priest who over the years had refined his science demonstrations down to the smallest detail; and they were presented with all the flare and precision of a Broadway show. His example of air pressure was especially memorable because he would place a marshmallow into a bell jar. Slowly he would pump out the air and the marshmallow, with less and less air pressing at its sides to help it hold its shape, would slowly begin to swell and expand. By the time most of the air had been taken out from the bell jar, the marshmallow looked as large as a rat. Then he would let in some air; and even that slight amount of air pressure was enough to make the marshmallow collapse into a gooey mess.

Among other scientific toys, he had a model rocket that whizzed across the physics lab. Rumor had it that when his assistant, who taught some of the other physics classes, broke the rocket, the good father locked the assistant out of the lab for the rest of the day.

However, like the good showman he was, he always saved the best for the climax, ending the final class with a bang. During the last day of instruction, he would set off a miniature replica of the atom bomb. There would be a bang and a flash of light and then a pillar of white dust would shoot up toward the ceiling where it spread out into the familiar mushroom shape.

Our lab reports had to be turned in on a special four-page cardboard form and in fountain pen ink. The report had to be thought out carefully in advance because it was impossible to erase any mistakes and no cross-outs were allowed. If you muffed the experiment itself, though, you could get a passing grade if you humbly wrote that you would have done better if you had followed his instructions. (However, that could be used as an excuse only once in the year so you still had to be careful in the lab. Like a "Get Out of Jail Free" card in Monopoly, you were wise to save that one for dire need.)

We also had an extraordinary chemistry teacher, a small, white-haired terrier of a man, who taught as a hobby rather than as a necessity. He had made a killing on the stock market with his knowledge of technology because he instantly grasped the money-making potential of a product. He had, I think, bought IBM and Xerox stock when they had first been offered and later invested in the Polaroid company. He only taught because he wanted to, not because he had to—which was just as well.

Our chemistry teacher was a smoker so it was hard on him that he could not smoke during school hours except in the teacher's room. As soon as the bell rang ending the last class, he would light up a cigarette. However, one day, early in his teaching career at St. Ignatius, he had poured that day's chemistry experiment down the drain and eagerly lit a cigarette. Without thinking, he tossed the match into the sink. The chemicals instantly caught fire and went racing through the school's plumbing. It was said that flames shot out of the basement toilets as if they were porcelain volcanoes—fortunately, they weren't occupied at the time of the eruptions. When the other teachers saw the flames coming out of the plumbing, they instinctively headed for the chemistry lab and our teacher.

His lectures were never dry, boring speeches because he always threw in stories of his adventures. As a young man, he had wandered up north where he had been an assayer—somebody who tests the purity of metals. Some days he had eaten whale blubber—which he said was delicious—because he had burned up so many calories that he needed to replace them quickly. However, almost every night he had slept on the bags of rock samples to make sure that no one made a switch.

In any event, I always looked forward to that particular class. He not only had a knack for making his lectures lively; but his demonstrations were equally entertaining.

When he was discussing liquid nitrogen, he put a half-dozen goldfish into a plastic bag and quick-froze them. To prove that they were frozen, he threw one against a wall where it shattered into a dozen little fish-bits that thawed into smelly pieces. The other, more fortunate, five were dropped into a goldfish bowl and allowed to thaw out there. I think three of them revived and were swimming around none the worse for wear.

Nor did he have trouble with discipline problems. If he thought we weren't paying enough attention, he would calmly step to the front of the lab, turn on a small electric fan to blow the fumes away from him and then set down a beaker with some chemical. Once, he used a type of acid which smells like vomit. Then he calmly went on lecturing while we began to gag. Since he had a regular arsenal of bad-smelling but harmless chemicals, he usually didn't have trouble with his classes.

From one of his favorite pranks in a restaurant, I learned how to make teaspoons that would dissolve in coffee—or anything else hot. I had to create a mold and then pour in a certain blend of metals with a low-boiling point. In his younger days, he used to like to switch his own spoon for the restaurant spoon, then stir it in the coffee which would melt the spoon. Then he would take a sip and spit it out, indignantly holding up the spoon and complaining in a loud voice to the rest of the restaurant that the coffee was too hot.

As a result, it was a pleasure to do extra credit work in chemistry. My own specialty was explosives. With a little practical chemistry, it's possible to make a bomb out of what you would find in most medicine cabinets. Among other things, he showed us how to make this marvelous paste which would not explode until it was dry. A bottle of it was dangerous; but a small amount was fun for practical jokes. It would go off with a bang like the smallest firecracker and perhaps sting the hand.

We smeared it all over the seat of this one classmate's desk and then waited expectantly. The victim strolled in without a worry on his mind and plopped down at his desk as he always did. There was a huge bang and he leapt out of his seat. At that point, we were still experimenting with the paste and making observations like good, budding scientists. We dutifully noted that we had used too much of the paste when we heard the loud BANG and the subject jumped up out of his seat. In fact, it hurt to sit down and he had to stand up for the rest of the class. Nor had anyone allowed for the fact that he would be wearing white jeans that were now stained a bright purple.

We became better at using the paste and also at defending ourselves. Once the paste had been set off, it wouldn't go off again so we soon learned to dust off desktops and seats and locker handles with our folders to set off any unexpected surprises. At the height of the madness, you could have seen a classroom of boys cautiously dusting off their desks like so many junior butlers.

However, like in any good Greek play, someone overreached

himself and put the paste on Father principal's doorknob. Father principal strolled down the hallway as he always did in his cassock and put his hand out to open his door as he did every day when it went off with a bang. Wringing his hand as if it had been slapped by a ruler, he knew immediately where to go—just as he had when the school toilets had caught fire. He stormed up the steps to the chem lab and informed our chemistry teacher that while it was fine to encourage young minds, he didn't have to encourage us *that* much and those particular set of experiments ended. However, I had done enough to win a science award when I graduated.

He also had a way of firing the imagination with the fortune waiting for the clever chemist. He was full of money-making ideas on a grand scale. A typical one was to develop a process to extract gold from the waters of the Pacific Ocean. Such a wild scheme might have made us laugh if it had come from someone else. However, we knew that his own futuristic vision had made him rich.

Because chemistry was not only profitable but fun, I fully intended to become a chemist as I headed into my senior year—a decision which pleased my father because he, too, had wanted to be a chemist before the Depression had forced him to drop out of junior college and take any job just to survive. I was going to be the one to learn how to skim gold from sea water.

Our school, however, was blessed with more than interesting science teachers; we also had excellent English teachers. In my senior year, we had Father Becker who taught us English by having us imitate the various writers and various forms. We had to write poems in the complicated rhyme scheme of the sestina; and we had to write scenes imitating Shakespeare. Our writing would never make anyone forget William or the other greats of English literature; but we learned the nuts and bolts of a style. To this day, I have to be careful what I read because I tend to imitate that writing.

Early in the semester, Father took some of us aside and said that if we wanted to get an "A" in his course, we would have to get something accepted by a national magazine. All of us were intimidated by the prospect; but in those days you didn't argue with a Jesuit priest—and you still don't. All of us tried. None of us got anything accepted; and he later retracted the threat and graded us by the same standards he used for the rest of the class. However, I got bitten by the bug and kept on trying.

I found that making up my own stories became as much fun as making explosives. Writing did not make a light bulb appear over my head. It did not make me scribble away in a frenzy as if I had just been zapped by an electric cattle prod. Nor was it a religious ecstasy. No symphony of cymbals crashed in climax when I reached the final paragraph.

Something else happened instead. Almost everyone I knew—whether they were white, yellow, or black—came from a single background. They were cut from one pattern of cloth. However, I was a bunch of different pieces that had been dumped together in a box by sheer circumstance.

I was the Chinese American raised in a black neighborhood, a child who had been too American to fit into Chinatown and too Chinese to fit in elsewhere. I was the clumsy son of the athletic family, the grandson of a Chinese grandmother who spoke more of West Virginia than of China.

When I wrote, I went from being a puzzle to a puzzle solver. I could reach into the box of rags that was my soul and begin stitching them together. Moreover, I could try out different combinations to see which one pleased me the most. I could take these different elements, each of which belonged to something else, and dip them into my imagination where they were melted down and cast into new shapes so that they became uniquely mine.

The first advice a beginning writer gets is to write about what you know; but that doesn't mean that the subject has to be in the same form you saw it. My first science-fiction novel, *Sweet-*

water, grew out of my memory of our living room in the Pearl Apartments. One day, as the light was rippling over the ceiling the way light reflects from the surface of a pool, I began to imagine what it would be like if the streets outside our apartment had been flooded—along with the rest of San Francisco.

My father, the kitemaker, became Windrider in *Dragonwings*. As I said, he had come to America at the age of ten but he did not like to talk much about the tough time he had had adjusting to life here. Writing *Dragonwings* was a way of stepping into his shoes.

My grandmother was the source of Paw-Paw in *Child of the Owl*—from her card playing and taste in radio stations to the layout of the apartment, as well as my other Chinatown landmarks. I once met a librarian and her daughter who had used the books as a kind of guidebook to Chinatown. With all the changes in Chinatown, that isn't possible anymore.

I used some of my own childhood for Craig Chin in *Sea Glass*.

Writing was, and still is, immensely satisfying. Bits and pieces, bits and pieces—all of them got put together in new and different, and I hoped, striking ways. However, I had as yet to get anything else but rejection letters—some of them nice and some of them not so nice.

All of that, though, was still ahead of me. I only knew that I enjoyed writing as much as I enjoyed science so that I was torn between majoring in chemistry and English in college.

At about that time, when I was trying to decide what to do with the rest of my life, my class went up to the wine country near St. Helena where there was a retreat house—a kind of dormitory where we could be led through several days of meditation. Up until then, our retreats had always been at school. We were expected to talk only at set times and let the priests guide our thoughts. So far, I had enjoyed them more as theater because our retreat masters were excellent at making their audience see and feel and hear what they were talking about—they could, if they wanted, make the pits of hell open up before us so that the flames would lick the soles of our feet.

This last retreat, though, I took more seriously because I had major decisions to make. In general, students got as much from that retreat as they put into it. Some students smuggled up six-packs of beer and used it as an excuse for a secret party. Others were more serious and read the religious literature left in our rooms and thought about God. My own experience fell somewhere between the sociable and the mystical.

I remember going for walks in the fields next to the dusty vineyards. In the daytime, the tall, golden weeds would crunch underneath my shoes and the air in front of me would be filled with pale, darting objects that were little grasshoppers trying to escape being crushed. Behind me, I left a trough like the frozen wake of a ship in a golden sea. At night, there would be all the stars overhead and the weeds glittering like silvery feathers.

At some time during these contemplative walks, I realized that I enjoyed making stories even more than making bombs. It was more of an impulse at that point in my life; but that is the way many self-truths reveal themselves—like a sprout germinating from a seed that has to work its way up through the dark soil and find a path that will lead it up from underneath a rock.

I think the sunshine and night sky also had something to do with my choice. Ironically, I decided that I didn't want to be locked up in a lab—little realizing how many sunny afternoons I would have to be stuck in my study because of a deadline on a story.

Before I went home, I tried to work out some of the mechanics of my decision because I didn't expect to make a living by writing stories. Instead, I thought I would try journalism first; and if that didn't work, I would teach English.

When I announced my ambition to my parents, they didn't object. If my father was disappointed, he hid it well. Most Chinese parents would have forced their son to go into some profession that would pay better than reporting or teaching. However, I was fortunate that mine gave me their full support.

As a result, when my teachers suggested I apply to the college of journalism at Marquette University, I did so. When I was accepted, I left for Milwaukee all set to undertake a career.

9

CULTURE SHOCK

IT WAS culture shock when I got off the plane. For one thing, Marquette was nothing like its brochure, which showed a campus of shady trees with quaint stone buildings. It was an urban campus that had spilled out of its original boundaries into the surrounding blocks. Hotels had been taken over and converted into dorms; and the area in general was going through redevelopment with more homeless people around than trees. The brochure photo had been cleverly shot to show the few trees on campus next to the St. Joan of Arc chapel—a medieval chapel imported onto campus stone by stone.

I had chosen Monitor Hall as my dorm because it was the only one that did not require a meal ticket. I was surprised when the taxicab driver pulled up in front of a dumpy three-story building; but the address was the correct one. It looked like a skid-row flophouse. The lobby was furnished with Salvation Army–style furniture, the floor was of no-nonsense concrete, and the ceilings were so low that sound echoed and reechoed. The only thing that separated it from a transient hotel was the bottle of emergency holy water on the second floor.

Just to the south was an industrial area nicknamed the Valley. It had grown up around a shipping channel connecting the Great Lakes with the sea; and it consisted of acres and acres of stained concrete and broken glass. Often, to get away from the campus, I would go for long walks there. Sometimes, though, if the wind was blowing wrong, we caught the stench from the tanning yard.

There was a telephone on each floor for incoming calls; but telephone service was often erratic whenever a little Irish lady ran the switchboard. She was an elderly woman with a strong Irish brogue who kept a glass of whiskey by the switchboard to keep her throat wet during her shift. Over the glass, she kept a holy card as if that were especially effective at keeping the smell of liquor from filling the lobby. People who made a call into the switchboard quickly learned to be polite to her because if she thought you needed a lesson in manners, she would wait until you and the caller had begun your conversation before she would cut in and shout, "Please."

I quickly got used to the Milwaukee dialect. Bubbler was a fountain. White soda, ironically, was 7UP. A basketball team didn't cream its opponent; instead it put the kibosh on them. I even got used to good "brats"—or bratwurst.

It was a little harder, though, getting used to Milwaukee itself, which I found sometimes to be a bit surrealistic. At about the time I arrived, the big thing had been running bootleg oleomargarine across the border from Illinois into Wisconsin. Because there were so many dairy farms in Wisconsin, the state wanted to encourage people to buy real butter rather than margarine. The laws were being changed around the time I was there; but for a long time it was illegal to sell colored margarine. If you bought margarine, you bought a kind of colorless lump into which you could mix your own yellow dyes. Since oleomargarine was cheaper than butter, our dorm chaplain, who also ran a school cafeteria, would drive down to Illinois and get colored oleomargarine and smuggle it back across the border.

However, I found most of my dormmates had that friendliness that is typical of the Midwest. I quickly learned how to play a kind of card game called Sheepshead and all-night games of Risk.

We also got caught up in playing practical jokes on one another. Somehow, one of us would get a key to our victim's room. Since every room had a sink, we removed the U-joint pipe beneath the sink and filled the basin with shaving cream. When the victim came into the room, the first thing he saw was the shaving cream in the sink. The natural reaction was to turn on the water without checking beneath the sink. The result was a flood of sudsy water that spread all over the room. Fortunately, the floor was made of concrete so that it only received a much-needed washing.

I also became good friends with a wide number of students, including the literary magazine editor, Joanne Ryder. Her Brooklyn accent made her seem like an exotic bird. I found her to be sweet, sensitive, and caring so that I could unburden some of my troubles to her. It was she who introduced me to the classics of children's literature, including *Winnie the Pooh* and the Narnia books; and I still have the copy of *Alice in Wonderland* she gave me.

More importantly, she helped broaden my personal horizons, exposing me to new ideas and attitudes. I came to think of her as a special friend.

At that time, though, my special buddy was a boy named Sam. Since we had no meal tickets, we often ate out together.

The cheapest meals were either pizza or meatball sandwiches from Angelo's; and we very quickly had our fill of both. The boys from Green Bay introduced us to Green Bay chili which consisted of a bowl of grease into which some spaghetti noodles and catsup (masquerading as spaghetti sauce) were tossed along with some mild chili and crushed oyster crackers. The resulting meal would sit like a rock in your stomach for hours, which was only useful if you were watching the "Pack," the Green Bay Packers, or ice fishing. Sometimes, though, we would treat ourselves by eating a five-course meal for $1.69 at a greasy spoon diner.

Our attempts at cooking for ourselves weren't much better. My brother had given me a hot plate he had used when we had been in college, so one day we had decided to cook Rice-a-Roni. Having no lid for the frying pan, I covered it with a *Time* magazine. When I finally took the magazine off, we found that the ink had run, dying the Rice-a-Roni pink. We still ate it anyway—it's amazing that we both survived our very first cooking lessons.

There was a Chinese restaurant on the same street as the Green Bay chili place. However, I quickly found they used American vegetables as substitutes for Chinese ones like *bok choy*—with celery and broccoli predominating. The ingredients were also cooked tourist style. Noodles were brown and crunchy, and the gravies were caramel colored. Nor was it very cheap. In terms of food value, the greasy spoon dive, which served five hamburgers for a dollar, was a better bargain.

The Chinese restaurant was run by two elderly Chinese who asked me to write my Chinese name down the first time I went in there. When they found out that I could not hold a conversation in Chinese, they retreated to the back and simply watched me while I ate. After years of run-ins with old-timers, I was wary of yet another sermon about learning Chinese or having them try to run my life as surrogate uncles and aunts. I was so uncomfortable that I did not eat there often.

However, there was one time when I would gladly have gone there. I loved movies; but there were only three movie theaters near campus—one of which was owned by the university so that it would run movies like *Arctic Adventure*. The two commercial theaters ran their selections for months so that for variety I wound up taking several buses to one of the outlying theaters to see a classic Japanese film. I don't remember the plot. I don't even remember the title. I just remember the five-course banquet in the movie that gave me a terrible case of the munchies—especially for anything that I could eat with a pair of chopsticks; but the Chinese restaurant was closed by then so I stopped by one of the few late-night delis and actually bought a can of Chung King chow mein and took it home to the dorm and used my hot plate.

As I grew more and more homesick, I must have groused more and more about Milwaukee—especially about how flat it was. Finally, to shut me up, a friend borrowed her aunt's car and took me out for a drive one night to show me the "hill." As we drove along, she explained how dangerous it was in the wintertime. Though kids used it for sledding, cars were always sliding back down its icy slopes. As she went on talking, the car gave a little jump as if it had gone over a bump. She turned and asked, "Did you feel it? Did you feel the hill?"

Of course, I had been looking forward to seeing snow. The first time I saw the white specks in the air, I thought someone's furnace was working wrong and sending white ash into the air. It wasn't until more had fallen that I realized it was snow. However, it didn't stay fluffy and white but soon turned into a gray, ugly slush.

Worse, no one told me about ice. Snow would fall. A thaw would partially melt it and then another spell of cold weather would freeze it. When more snow fell, it became a regular trap for a Californian. As I was shivering and continually falling, winter soon lost any appeal for me. To add insult to injury, Sam went out and bought a derby jacket. I considered that standard summer wear for San Francisco; but he considered it warm enough for heavy winter. In general, winter only made Milwaukee seem more surreal because there was a gas station down the way with a lawn of astroturf. During a temporary thaw, they would clean their lawn by hosing the slush from the green astroturf.

In general, Milwaukee and Marquette were both stuck a decade behind the rest of the country. I once marched with some friends to demonstrate for more black professors on the faculty. There were about a hundred of us or so. As we began to walk, we noticed police on foot and on motorcycles at every intersection. In fact, there were more police than demonstrators.

While most of America was debating about the Vietnam War and civil rights, the biggest demonstration at Marquette was for the resumption of football.

Besides being homesick, I was beginning to feel a new sense of alienation. Out of some twenty thousand students, I doubt if there were more than a hundred who were not white—and a number of these were members of the basketball team. St. Ignatius had been almost all white; but there was always my family and Chinatown to fall back on. In Milwaukee there was only a laundry and the Chinese restaurant; and yet I was uneasy enough about myself to avoid the restaurant.

Nor was I doing well in journalism. I hit rock bottom that winter when I was supposed to write an article about buses. I stood on a winter corner, shivering for an hour so I would have enough material for writing; but wound up getting an "F" because I put the turn signals too high up on the bus. One of my journalism teachers even suggested that I had more of a talent for fiction than for fact—which has ironically turned out to be prophetic.

Besides the shock of getting an "F"—when I had been used to getting "A's"—I also felt as if I were wasting my parents' money. My parents were going through various economies, both big and small, to pay the high tuition, room, and board at Marquette. Among the personal sacrifices, my father even gave up drinking any soda to save money. Remembering his own disappointments, he had also taken out a special kind of college loan from the bank. If anything had happened to my parents, I would still receive enough money to complete my college education.

I found myself turning inward. Stuck physically in Milwaukee, I could only go back to San Francisco in my imagination. Up until then I had been writing contemporary realistic stories and sending those off—receiving rejection letters in return. I finally decided to write a science-fiction story.

It seems so obvious that I should have been trying science fiction from the very beginning. I liked the genre and I also liked science; but part of the writing process is finding the best way to express yourself as a writer. The Irish writer, George Bernard Shaw, wrote several mediocre novels until he finally decided to try plays and became famous for writing those. His most famous play, *Pygmalion*, eventually became the Broadway and movie hit *My Fair Lady*.

In any event, I sat down and began to write a story about a time when San Francisco had fallen into the sea during an earthquake. The hero of the story goes back to the ruins to try to discover his roots. He thinks he's a human but discovers that he's an alien.

Having written my first science-fiction story, "The Selchey Kids," I decided to submit it to one of the science-fiction magazines I enjoyed reading. I sent off that story and to my surprise I sold it, receiving a penny a word which is what Charles Dickens got in his day—though pennies went further in his day. Eventually the story was included in the *World's Best Science Fiction of 1969*.

Naturally I began to write more science fiction; and in looking back at those early stories, I was writing either about alienated heroes or aliens—even trying to tell the alien's viewpoint in the first person. All those years I had been trying to solve puzzles when the biggest puzzle had been myself.

I sent out more science-fiction stories and got more rejection slips than acceptances. On one story returned by a famous science-fiction editor, the words, "Who Cares?" had been written. Another rejected a story because I wrote "awful purple prose" and requested that I not send him anymore. The fact that I kept writing—and publishing, though not with them— is a testament to perseverance.

About three years after I had sold my first story, my college friend Joanne, who by then had joined the children's department at Harper & Row, asked me to write something for children, so I wrote a children's science-fiction novel, *Sweetwater*.

My relationship with Joanne was very similar to the situation in the movie, *When Harry Met Sally*. We began as friends and fell in love. Over the years as my wife, she has continued to be my best friend, adviser, and inspirer. It's hard for two writers to work at home when both need privacy; but we've tried to deal with it by having separate studies. Again, it's hard to schedule things together because one can never be sure how long a writing session will last. In general, we try to have one meal together—whether it's breakfast, lunch, or dinner. Often, we toss off ideas to one another. Other times we sympathize with one another's problems, including the time Joanne wanted to dedicate *Night Flight* to me but there was so much text and so many pictures that there wasn't room for a separate dedication page. Joanne and her editor, the resourceful Meredith Charpentier, solved it by putting the dedication as graffiti on the base of a statue in a park on the opening spread.

It's strange to be a unit when two people can be so different. I like movies; Joanne likes nature walks. I collect lead soldiers; Joanne likes flower arranging. And yet it would be difficult to think of life without her.

10
MY BROOKLYN GRANDMOTHER

MEMORIES are like apple seeds. Plant a seed from a McIntosh apple and you might get a tree that grows a Delicious instead. Apple seeds do not grow "true" as they say. In order to get new McIntosh trees, a farmer must graft buds from old McIntosh trees onto young apple trees.

However, what is bad for an orchardist is not necessarily bad for a writer. Memories fall like so many seeds into the imagination where they germinate in their own rhythm and timing; and it doesn't matter if they do not grow exactly as the original. In fact, if the harvest is to be special, it's sometimes better if they don't grow "true."

When I wrote *Sweetwater*, I wrote about aliens called Argans. At the time that I was creating the race, it felt somehow right to say that they were all uncles, nephews, and cousins; but I couldn't say why it felt correct.

It was only later when I began writing *Dragonwings* and had to re-create the Chinatown of the 1900s that I understood why. In the nineteenth century because of the various immigration laws, it was difficult if not impossible for a Chinese man to bring his wife and children to America. As a result, though these men were married and had families, they lived most of their lives as bachelors. Of course, in an American Chinatown, they would all be uncles, nephews, and cousins to someone because it would be mostly men living there. Any family relationships would be male.

In writing about alienated people and aliens in my science fiction, I was writing about myself as a Chinese American. In *Dragonwings*, some of the old-timers I had known in Chinatown became Uncle Bright Star and the other members of the laundry company. Again, some of my cousins used to debate about who was the model for Phil the Pill in *Child of the Owl*. Some of my Uncle Quail's crustiness came from my Uncle Francis.

Nor can you expect memories to germinate as quickly as apple seeds. Memories sprout at their own time and pace. When I first read about the early Chinese-American aviator, Fung Joe Guey, I could see his airplane turning over the hilltop. So I put that scene down on paper. However, it took me four years to explain why he was on top of that hill—and why he had built the airplane in the first place.

It took even longer for Uncle Bright Star's story to grow. At about the same time I wrote about airplane flight, I also wrote a scene of a Chinese boy shivering in the snows of the Sierras. It's taken some twenty years to figure out how and why he got there; and it's required two other books, *Serpent's Children* and *Mountain Light* to set up the background.

The long period for growth is sometimes partially due to the research. To create the Chinatown of *Dragonwings*, I had to write about the Chinatown of the early 1900s, which meant I had to find enough information about that time period to make the setting authentic. Imagine that you have to build a house out of toothpicks. However, the toothpicks themselves are scattered through several libraries in several cities, so before you can begin building, you have to pick up the toothpicks one at a time. That was similar to what I had to do with *Dragonwings*, picking up one piece of information here and another piece there.

Nor does the tree always grow from the ground up. Sometimes a book develops in reverse from branch to root rather than from root to branch as you would expect. *Dragonwings*, as I said, grew from the scene of the airplane flight which forms one of the last chapters in the book. So most of the four years was spent writing the chapters that came before the scene. (In general, I've found that it's best to work with a scene that I feel strongly about. The process of writing a novel can take so long that only the strongest material can fuel the imagination over a lengthy period.)

I can also never be sure where a story will take me. *Dragon of the Lost Sea* began as a picture book in which the Monkey King captured a cruel spirit with a trick. However, I kept asking myself what had driven the spirit to her evil deeds in the first place so that the picture book finally grew into a conventional fantasy novel in which children from our ordinary world are taken into another universe. I had already done several complete drafts and thought I finally had a manuscript that was ready to be submitted; but toward the end of that version there was a special pair—a dragon and her boy—who stole the scene whenever they were on stage. I realized that I had to scrap what I had done and begin over again; and it's now taken me three more books to finish the story—*Dragon Steel*, *Dragon Cauldron*, and *Dragon War*. At any rate, it took me four novels to do what other people do in eight pages of text. It wasn't simply writing the story but creating the universe of the books that I've come to enjoy. And they provided a special refuge after my father's death in 1989.

By now, I know I can finish a book when I have two things: a piece of music and a narrative voice. I usually write to music that I listen to over headphones, which helps shut me off from doorbells ringing, phones jangling, and noise from the street that might distract me. I wore out one record of Copland's Clarinet Concerto writing *Sweetwater*. *Dragonwings** was written to Ralph Vaughan Williams, and the Mark Twain books—*The Mark Twain Murders* and *The Tom Sawyer Fires*—were written to the B-52s.

The voice is also important since I usually like to write a first-person narrative. However, even if I tell a story in the third person, there is usually one character to act as a focus for the viewpoint. I once heard an actor say that whatever role he's playing acts as a lens for all of his experience that day—not just when he's on stage. When he's Willy Loman in *Death of a Salesman*, he can see other people's pain. When he's Iago in *Othello*, he always wonders what is the other person's angle.

Something similar happens when I find a narrative voice. I start to settle into that character—which sometimes makes it difficult for my long-suffering wife. Joanne particularly disliked it when I was writing about Shimmer the dragon because the "dragon" in me would also come out.

Sometimes my readers tell me that they can't be writers because nothing special happens to them. Keeping your eyes open is the key to being a writer. Anything you see could provide the seed for a story some day. Once, up in Seattle, I was talking to a group of children. Among other things, I brought up the Godzilla movies and said that I was worried there weren't going

*This book was written appropriately enough to the musical version of *I Remember Mama*. The television show was a special favorite of our entire family.

to be any more good ones because I heard the actor who played Godzilla was retiring.

A little boy piped up from the back of the room, "You mean there's an actor who plays Godzilla?"

I felt as if I had killed Santa Claus and the Easter Bunny all in one blow. However, the experience stayed with me and eventually grew into *Kind Hearts and Gentle Monsters*. (The original title was *Yes, Virginia, There Is a Godzilla* but we couldn't get permission from the Japanese film studios to use Godzilla in the title.)

During my early years of writing, one of the strongest influences on my life had been my grandmother; and it was inevitable that she should also affect my writing

As I said, she lived in Brooklyn Place so that I sometimes thought of her as my Brooklyn grandmother. I didn't always know what to make of my grandmother; and I don't think she always knew what to make of me. We were like two wrestlers on a slippery mat where the true victory would have lain in a mutual embrace that would have supported one another; but it was as if we were oiled, our hands slipping even as we tried to grip one another.

Most of the time, though, it didn't matter how different I was. She accepted her Americanized grandchild; and the way she expressed that love was with food. As the youngest, I would often be seated next to her at a family banquet so she would, of course, heap my plate with food. If I didn't clear the plate, she was bound to think something was wrong with the food. So I would dutifully make my way through the pile of food. However, if I made the mistake of turning to say something to someone else, I would find the plate heaped up once again. Eating with my grandmother took a certain amount of concentration.

My grandmother had become a great cook; and, like any good cook, my grandmother was careful about her praise. The highest compliment she gave to another cook was to allow how Auntie Mary's cooking wasn't bad.

Like all good cooks, my grandmother was especially particular about the ingredients. For one thing, she preferred small sweet potatoes, eating those with gusto. She was fussiest, though, about rice.

One day she asked me to help her in the kitchen—which was her way of saying that she was going to teach me. First, she announced, we were going to wash the rice. In the old days, washing rice was wise because I'm told they used talcum on the grains. Even now, its wise to wash the rice at least once to see what might come up.

My grandmother had me pour lukewarm water into a pot of rice and swirl my hand around in it. Instantly the water turned milky; and she had me look alertly for stray bits of chaff or even the occasional pebble that might slip by the processing machines.

Then, setting the lid over most of the pot, I had to pour the water out gently. However, when I asked her what the next step was, she told me that the rice wasn't clean yet and to refill the pot with lukewarm water and repeat the process. By the sixth time, the water was clear no matter how often I swirled my hand around. Even then, that wasn't enough. I remember my fingers were wrinkled by the time she declared the dirt was gone—as were most of the vitamins and nutritional elements as well.

My grandmother, like most experienced cooks, never used exact measurements. It was a pinch of this or a handful of that. When she had me add water the final time, she rested her fingertip on the surface of the rice until the water came up almost to the knuckle of her index finger. Then the rice was allowed to soak for a half-hour before cooking. The rice was brought to a boil, stirred once with a spoon, and then allowed to simmer for twenty minutes. The result was rice of just the right consistency and density.

Along with the cooking lessons, some of my grandmother's own personality soaked into me. I've never been able to abide instant rice—which tastes mushy to me. Brown rice tastes musty; and I've never been able to get the hang of a modern rice cooker. Instead, I still make rice basically the way my grandmother showed me, even to measuring the water in the pot with a knuckle—though I only wash the rice once now. I think some of the fussiness over the rice carries over into my writing forcing me to write several drafts of a book before I'm satisfied.

As expressions of her love, she kept me well supplied with what I used to call potato chip fish but which was really called *dai day*, salted sand dabs, a small flat fish from Monterey that I have never been able to find since the Chinese fishing colony there disappeared. The flesh was denser and saltier than regular salted fish, *hom yee*.

However, it was something as humble and homely and unlikely as the taro root that called out the artist in her. She made many tasty and delightful dishes out of taro root. But I especially remember how she would take a taro root, cut a slender thread from it, and skillfully turn the root, making the thread grow longer until she had enough to make a small ball. In to this would go onions and bits of meat; and she would deep fry the whole concoction.

Later, when I had left San Francisco to go to college, she always sent me boxes of special treats, from my favorite cookies to preserved plums to *lop cheong*—the latter of which I cooked on a hot plate with rice in my dorm room. Much to my delight, her care packages followed me all across America.

I never told her how much she meant to me; and yet trying to come to grips with her meant coming to grips with myself and that "Chineseness."

In some ways I was like the artist, Ed Young, the creator of the Caldecott-winning *Lon Po Po*, who once told me of his own attempt to become an American. When Ed came to America from Shanghai, he wanted to become an American in the worst way. As he once told me, as soon as he had arrived here, he signed up for the first three courses he could take at San Francisco City college—they were beginning, intermediate, and advanced typing all in the same semester.

By the time he moved east and began teaching art, he was thoroughly Americanized. However, at about that time, his knees began to hurt. None of the regular doctors could cure him. Finally, someone told him about this "quaint" doctor of herbalism in New York's Chinatown. At this point, in constant pain and ready to try anything, he went to the herbal doctor.

The "quaint" doctor turned out to be Professor Cheng, the master of the five excellences (medicine, tai chi chuan, painting, poetry, and calligraphy) and the youngest professor at Beijing University. Between tai chi chuan and his medicines, he managed to cure Ed. Ed realized that he would never meet another person like this extraordinary man. After some hesitation, he gave up his art career and became the full-time interpreter for Professor Cheng for several years. It was only when his master died that Ed resumed his artistic career, much the stronger for it.

When I finally decided to try to confront my own "Chineseness," I wanted to do so in company with my grandmother—if only in my imagination. I began to write about a Chinese-American girl who has to live with her grandmother in Chinatown. For the first time in her life, the girl has to confront being Chinese. In that original draft, the grandmother had a pet cat named after an emperor of China, so I entitled it, *The Emperor of China Only Has One Ear*.

However, in looking around, I realized there was a spate of books about ghetto children and stray cats so I chucked the pet figuratively out the window and changed the story line so that it eventually became *Child of the Owl*. Even after it was published and began to receive honors like *Dragonwings*, I still didn't tell my grandmother how much of an inspiration she had been to me. I simply gave her a copy that she kept with the other books I had written.

If this was a movie, we would stop now when *Dragonwings* and *Child of the Owl* started to win awards. All problems are supposed to end at that point; but an incident happened which put everything into perspective. Because of it, I'm still pleased when a book is given a prize; but I know now that it is the book that receives it rather than me. I learned to take my writing seriously but not myself; and that insight was the last lesson—and gift—my grandmother gave me.

Toward the end of her life, her health began to fail; and she was in and out of hospitals. At one point, her doctor checked her into French Hospital out toward the ocean. To everyone's distress there, she only picked at her meals. Family, nurses, doctors, and the dietician were all worried about her loss of appetite. Finally, one day my mother, my Auntie Mary, and I happened to be visiting her during lunchtime. When the nurse brought in her lunch, my grandmother stared in exasperation at the sandwich. Raising one corner of the bread to reveal the white meat, my grandmother complained that all they gave her was turkey in one form or another.

Now my grandmother hated turkey, claiming that it gave her diarrhea. Every Thanksgiving, my mother would roast a chicken for my grandmother in addition to a turkey for the rest of us. Nowadays, the area around French Hospital is mainly Asian; but when my grandmother was there, the area was still mostly white and so were most of the patients. As a result, the hospital menu reflected white tastes.

This gave me a chance to pay her back a little bit for all that she had done and to express my love for her in the same language she used—food. What small amount of fame I had received was useless in this context. The "famous" writer was as helpless as anyone else. At that moment, getting my starving grandmother to eat counted for far more than any honors I'd been awarded for my writing. Suddenly, the prizes were put into their proper perspective: While they were good for inflating egos and swelling heads, there were many things for which they were ineffective—like saving someone you loved.

Determined to find some Chinese food for her, I set out. However, as I walked around the white neighborhood, I began to despair. Then, just when I was about to turn back, I found a Chinese delicatessen that was pioneering in the area. Lying in a metal pan in the window was a steamed chicken, complete with head and beak. It was something as bland as any dietician could have wanted, so I went inside.

That brought me to my next trial: my first attempt at shopping for Chinese food by myself. Up until then, I had always gone with someone else who could do the ordering—either my grandmother or my mother. For me, it was as nervewracking a moment as the first time I drove a car by myself.

I tried to remember the Chinese words my grandmother had used when she purchased a chicken; but I could not so I simply pointed at it. Then I used the one Chinese phrase I remembered which was to cut it up, emphasizing the idea by pantomiming a cleaver chopping. It was with no small feeling of triumph that I watched as the clerk behind the counter grunted and did as I had requested.

With the container concealed under my coat, I stole back into the hospital. After the room and hallway were clear of nurses, I snuck the carton out of my coat and handed it to my grandmother. When she raised the flaps, she had the same delighted expression that I used to have back east when I had opened up her care packages.

As I stood in the doorway to keep watch, my grandmother devoured most of the chicken. In truth, it may have been her first real meal in several days. When she was finished, we put the bones back into the carton so I could take away the evidence.

Then, so she wouldn't get in trouble with the dietician and nurses, she made my mother and my aunt eat the turkey sandwich. Like a good mother, she gave each of her daughters a half so they wouldn't quarrel.

II

SEEDS

MEMORIES are like seeds. They lie concealed within the imagination—or perhaps they are buried even deeper, ripening with the quickening of the heart and growing according to the soul's own season. Planted in childhood, they sometimes do not bear fruit until long into adulthood. However, even if they lie sleeping within the imagination, within the heart, within the soul, they do not perish.

Back in 1951, during Uncle Francis's wanderings, he and his wife, my Auntie Rachel, and their family wound up in West Virginia. The laundry in Clarksburg had been torn down to make a parking lot for Union National Bank—my family seems to have an affinity for future parking lot sites.

However, my mother's family had also lived for a time in the neighboring town of Bridgeport prior to their departure to California. Since my mother and Auntie Rachel had left Bridgeport as children, neither could remember the address of their old home; and yet once she was in that town, Auntie Rachel was able to trace her way back to the house.

Climbing the steps to the porch, my aunt knocked at the front door. When it was opened, she introduced herself to the present occupants of her old house. She chatted with them for a bit before they asked her if she would explain something that had been puzzling them for over twenty years. Taking her into the backyard, they showed her a particularly tenacious weed that they had been trying to get rid of for decades. They had chopped it with hoes, dosed it with herbicide, and dug up its roots with spades. However, the plant kept growing back as if it were determined to stay.

It turned out to be a Chinese vegetable that my grandparents had planted so long ago. It had transplanted well from China to America, exasperating a generation of gardeners.

It may be something as simple and yet as indestructible as a weed that links us to our past and binds us to our dreams. Seeds, cast into strange soil, may thrive and grow—just like children and just like their memories.

Memory never quite goes away. It is there, only hidden, like the laughter of unseen children in a garden. A home can be cemented over but never buried. Adults can put up steel and lay asphalt, but their buildings and streets can never outlast memory. Memory pays no rent and is assessed no taxes, yet its value is infinite.

I go to the gate of the garage and I peer through the heavy metal bars at the oil-stained cement, trying to see where my father's garden once was. It was a simple garden for a simple man: one fuchsia plant and crates of dirt on top of benches improvised from boards and hundred-pound rice cans. The sunlight entered the garden only for an hour a day; but the plants grew. The cats came, delighted to find flowers in the middle of that asphalt jungle.

Cement covers where the garden once was; and yet I know that below the steel I-beams, beneath the concrete, in the midst of the moist, sandy soil, the seeds from that garden lie waiting. And I also know that some of those seeds are already sprouting, rising through the darkness, through the earth, through steel and cement to emerge into the light.

I look through the gate of the parking garage not at what is there now but at what was there before—and what is now within me. . . . Within my imagination, within my heart, within my soul, I feel the seeds of that garden stirring.

AFTERWORD

I HAVE changed the names of my classmates because I imagine that they don't want their children to know what they've done. I have felt a similar obligation to leave out the names of some of my teachers and neighbors.

A word of thanks is also due Sally Foxen for all her help.

Best in biography and autobiography from BEECH TREE BOOKS

Anne Frank: Life in Hiding
by Johanna Hurwitz

Anonymously Yours
by Richard Peck

Behind the Border
by Nina Kossman

But I'll Be Back Again
by Cynthia Rylant

Dear Dr. Bell … Your Friend, Helen Keller
by Judith St. George

E. B. White: Some Writer!
by Beverly Gherman

Harriet: The Life and World of Harriet Beecher Stowe
by Norma Johnston

In Kindling Flame: The Story of Hannah Senesh, 1921–1944
by Linda Atkinson

The Invisible Thread
by Yoshiko Uchida

The Life and Death of Martin Luther King, Jr.
by James Haskins

Louisa May: The World and Works of Louisa May Alcott
by Norma Johnston

The Moon & I
by Betsy Byars

The Road from Home: The Story of an Armenian Girl
by David Kherdian